OUT OF DARKNESS

{A Spiritual Approach to Inner Darkness and Pain}

Bernard Hayes, C.R.

Printed in Canada

FIN 09 03 06

Library and Archives Canada Cataloguing in Publication

Hayes, Bernard

Out of darkness / Bernard Hayes.

ISBN 0-9780213-0-4

1. Suffering--Religious aspects--Christianity. 2. Psychic trauma--Religious aspects--Christianity. I. Title.

BV4909.H387 2006   248.8'6   C2006-901141-9

Contents

*I dedicate this book to all who, in loving me,
have helped to heal me.*

Acknowledgements

Some words of thanks are definitely in order. I offer them first of all to the many people who have been of invaluable assistance to me in my own wrestling. Thanks also to Gregory Stanley-Horn, Reverend Charles Fedy, CR and John Brothers for their helpful suggestions. Special acknowledgements go to Pamela Mank of the Catholic Family Counselling Centre in Kitchener, Ontario. Without her expert help and her loving encouragement, I doubt this book would have ever been completed. Sincere thanks also to the professional staff at the Southdown Institute in Aurora, Ontario for the expert care and concern they so genuinely give to all who seek their help. Lastly, to Jennifer Berry whose technical expertise was invaluable.

Dear Reader,

It is my hope that as you read these pages you will take time to reflect on them in the light of your own life situation so that we may together accomplish the healing they are intended to bring.

No single book of this nature can speak specifically to all situations. We are individuals and we all respond to our lives in very personal ways. No two lives ever follow the same identical path.

Many of us today live with what often are excessive demands on our time and energy. I have tried to be very aware of this in writing this book. I have, therefore, deliberately kept each chapter as concise as possible.

You will find some repetition in these pages. There is a reason for this. Often the obstacles to self-healing are so strong they can only be dealt with effectively by repeated and repetitive self-reinforcement.

Much of the material we will deal with finds its roots in a series of sins which are known as the Capital Sins. The word "capital" comes from a Latin word which means "head" or "source". These sins (lust, gluttony, pride, etc.) are seen as the source of the evil in us and around us. They are intertwined and operate in conjunction with one another. Therefore the healing approach to one is often the same as the healing approach to another.

Finally, if what I have written proves to be of help to even a single person, the book will have fulfilled its purpose.

Bernard Hayes, C.R.
January 5, 2006

Introduction

We are becoming more and more familiar with the term "inner demons." We all have some. They are part and parcel of who we are as humans and we need to deal with them if we are to live healthy lives physically, emotionally and spiritually. They are the inner voices that drive us to those compulsive behaviour patterns that have the power to destroy us. Sometimes they exercise their power periodically, over shorter periods or longer periods in our lives. Sometimes they take complete possession of us. In either case, as long as they are in charge we know them best as "addictions."

Addictions come in many forms. They can be life-long or restricted to certain times in our lives.

When we think of or talk about addictions, we are most often thinking of some form of chemical addiction (drugs; alcohol, etc.) But we can also be addicted in other ways, which are less obvious but equally destructive.

In his paper "The Roots of Addiction in Free Market Society," psychologist Bruce Alexander has stressed the destructiveness of non-chemical addiction. Dr. Alexander is a Professor of Psychology at Simon Fraser University and a Research Associate with the Canadian Centre for Policy Alternatives. He writes;

> The word "addiction has come to be narrowly applied to excessive drug use in the 20th century, but historically it was applied to non-drug habits as well. There is ample evidence that sever addictions to non-drug habits are every bit as dangerous and

resistant to treatment as drug addictions, whether they be the compulsion for money, power, work, food, material goods, or perfection.

Addiction in the modern world can be best understood as a compulsive lifestyle that people adopt in desperation as a substitute when they are dislocated from the myriad intimate ties between people and groups – from the family, to the spiritual community – that are essential for every person in every type of society.

It is these addictions that are the subject of this book.

While medical and psychotherapeutic treatments often do have a certain level of success in dealing with addictions, it is my contention that the full and comprehensive handling of many addictions demands that we give equal emphasis to our need for spiritual healing. A great deal of our addictive behaviour is triggered by more than a physical need. Very often the root-cause lies in some need for inner or spiritual healing. That is the approach I am taking.

I believe this approach is valid since unhealthy addictions inevitably lead to actions that are sinful and sin can only effectively be dealt with in the realm of the spiritual. More about this later.

Writing this book has been a combination of "difficult" and "easy." It has been difficult because of the complexity of the material. It has been easy because so much of what is said here comes from my own lived experience and that of others I have counselled. The more I continue to try to provide the spiritual counsel many seek, the more I become convinced of how much help is needed.

As a Christian, my spiritual approach is based in Christian tradition and teaching. It is my contention, however, that these resonate in significant ways with those of many religious traditions and will not seriously conflict with any. My hope, therefore, is that this material will be of help to believers across a wide and varied spectrum.

As pain-filled as it may prove to be, self-examination is an indispensable requisite for personal integration and growth. Only when we honestly acknowledge and confront the demons who dwell in our darkness can we even begin the struggle that will make us whole.

PART 1: PREPARING TO WRESTLE

Chapter 1: Wrestling

"Where does evil come from? It is in each of us. Each of us has to face it, own it, deal patiently with it."
(Grover Gauntt – Buddhist Monk reflecting on The Holocaust.)

When I was deciding on a title for this book, I debated a long time about using that word, "wrestling." No other word better expresses the reality of our struggle with our demons. The fact is that we never really completely overcome them or totally conquer them once and for all. All we can hope to do is get the upper hand and bring them under our control. That is what a successful wrestler does: he wrestles his opponents to the mat and brings them under his control.

The fact is though that wrestling isn't too popular a sport in our society – genuine wrestling anyway. It takes time and planning and strategy. It can be drawn out, not very exciting, even boring. It doesn't fit with our fast-paced, immediate reward mentality.

Wrestling demands patience and patience just isn't part of our make-up. Our social conditioning gears us to impatience. We can't wait for anything and we can't put up with anything for very long. We live in a culture of "instant": instant coffee, instant meals, instant cures, instant perfection. We want what we want when we want it and, if it doesn't come that quickly, we either force it to happen or we let it go. Our standard for action seems to be: if it takes time, it's not worth the effort. All of that makes "wrestling" rather repugnant.

Like it or not, however, the reality is that we can't avoid wrestling. We all struggle with some things (physical, emotional or spiritual) for our entire lives. And if these things are not going to defeat us, if we want to deal with them in non-destructive ways, we must learn to be patient with ourselves and others – as patient as God and others are with us.

The first obstacle then to effectively dealing with our

inner demons is our ingrained impatience. The second is our unwillingness to suffer.

Even though we want (sometimes desperately) to deal with our demons, we all too often look at the time and suffering that will be involved and we turn away. We want desperately to bring the demon under control – but only if we can do so quickly and, perhaps even more importantly, without pain.

Like our impatience, our deep aversion to suffering is a result of our social conditioning. We live in a society where suffering has become a dirty word, something to be avoided like the plague. All it is for us is an unwelcome, unproductive hindrance in our lives. We don't see its value and therefore, in our minds, it has no value. In the minds of many, the only people who embrace it or see value in it are religious freaks. Sensible people avoid it at all costs.

Our approach to suffering is both regrettable and destructive. It divorces us from the reality of life and deprives us of suffering's gift: the gift of our own growth. I am not trying to glorify suffering. In and of itself suffering is neither glorious, nor glamorous. People who seek suffering for its own sake are in a pitiable psychological state. Undoubtedly, we are justified in seeking legitimate relief from suffering, especially when it is brought about by circumstances beyond our control or by others who act unjustly or abusively towards us.

Not all suffering, however, falls into these categories. Much of our suffering arises directly from our lives. Throughout our lives we may be plagued with suffering arising from chronic illness, mental or physical disabilities, severe emotional dysfunction, the heartbreaks others cause us or we cause ourselves, etc. There is often little or nothing we can do to permanently remove or even ease that suffering. It becomes part and parcel of our lives.

The same is not necessarily true of the suffering we inflict on ourselves by our chosen lifestyles. At least at certain stages these can be dealt with and a degree of healing achieved.

All types of suffering have something in common. All call us to growth, to self-purification, to cleanse ourselves of our self-delusions, our shame and pretense, and force us to be real. This can change us for the better. There is a great example of this in the Book of Genesis from the Old Testament.

The central theme of Genesis is God creating, not just our universe, but ourselves as well. And His work of creating is never finished. He is constantly re-creating both our world and us, refining His creation so that more and more it fulfills its intended purpose.

One of the central stories in the Book of Genesis is that of Jacob and his older brother, Esau. Jacob is possessed by envy and resentment (hatred) against Esau because Esau will inherit everything from their father and Jacob will be left with nothing. Jacob is his mother's favourite son. So he and his mother devise a rather sordid plot to rob Esau of the inheritance and ensure that it goes to Jacob. The scheme works but the result is a disastrous rift between the two brothers.

Eventually Jacob repents and sets out on a journey to reconcile with Esau. On the way, however, he is met by a being with whom he is forced to wrestle. The match results in a draw, but Jacob is left with a physical deformity and a changed name. He is also a changed man. His envy has been controlled and he is now much better equipped to fulfill God's purpose for him (Gen. 27, 1 - 43 and 32, 23 - 31)

This story is one of many accounts that can introduce us to a whole new dimension in our struggle with suffering. It can help us to see our suffering, not as God's punishment, but as part of his loving design for us. In our suffering God calls us to become more and more fully the beauty he intended us to be when he created us.

The great English Christian author, C.S. Lewis, expressed this aspect of suffering very beautifully in his book, The Problem of Pain. He compared God to a great artist. If a master painter is to paint a picture for a child, he very quickly dashes one off and gives it to the child. But, when the artist comes to paint his masterpiece, he takes great pain. He paints and rubs out time and again. And, if his canvas could feel, it would suffer with every rubbing. But also with every rubbing, it would become more and more fully the masterpiece the artist hopes it will be. And, says Lewis, we are God's masterpiece – each of us!

As difficult and unpleasant as they are, patience and suffering are essential weapons in our wrestling with our inner demons. Furthermore, if their effectiveness is to be complete, we must cultivate them in accordance with the totality of our being, both emotionally and spiritually. Neither will be sufficient alone. True holistic healing will address our entire self, body and soul. We are neither only one, nor only the other. We are both.

Chapter 2: Body and Soul

"Your opponent, the devil, is prowling about like a roaring lion looking for someone to devour." (1 Peter 5, 8)

Whenever healing is needed, humankind has always acknowledged the need to heal the soul as well as the body. It is a process still reflected in the healing practices and rites of many cultures, even in this modern day. Only in the predominant culture of the Western world with its intense and exaggerated emphasis on a scientific approach to life has this union been diminished or dismissed.

With increasing understanding, however, many modern medical practitioners are again acknowledging that the connection between the body and soul is an essential component in all complete health care. More and more they are acknowledging that true holistic healing must deal with healing the inner person as well as the mind and body.

Dr. Christina Pulchaski is a modern pioneer practitioner in this field. In 2001 she established the Institute for Spiritual Care at the George Washington University in the United States. It is based on the concept that "spirituality is a key dimension for achieving optimal health and coping with illness."

So far, 122 U.S. medical schools have developed programmes in keeping with the Institute's purpose. It has also been introduced at the University of Saskatchewan in Canada.

Doctor Pulchaski believes that health care practitioners have an "ethical obligation" to treat the whole person and to respond to all their needs including their spiritual needs. Her definition of spiritual needs includes organized religion, but also takes in to account the need to respond to the needs of secular patients and atheists by dealing with those things that give meaning to their lives.

The validity of the programme has been bolstered by a national mental health survey conducted in 2001. The survey concluded that at least 43 percent of those surveyed used prayer as an adjunct to doctor's help.

Given the ingrained caution of the medical profession, progress in this area will undoubtedly be slow. It is, however, being introduced into more and more medical schools in spite of some resistance. This resistance is usually caused by the misperception that the programme is designed to promote one religion or to proselytize. Once it is made clear that this is not the case, opposition melts away.

My own experience puts me firmly in the holistic healing camp. Words like "soul" and "spirit" may have different meanings at different times and for different people but none of us can reasonably deny that we are more than flesh and bone or brain and emotions. There is in each of us some inner person: some inner reality that makes you uniquely you and me uniquely me. For many of us that inner person, our non-material or spiritual interior reality, is what we are referring to when we talk of the soul. And, it is there that our inner addictive voices reside and the base from which they operate.

A word about "demons" is in order here.

Often when we are frightened of something or simply want to dismiss it we make it an object of ridicule, something we can have a good laugh at. The more unreal and ridiculous we can make what we fear, the less we have a reason to fear it and the more we can control it. We have done that with Satan (the Devil). After all, who can take seriously an ugly creature with a tail running around with a pitchfork?

The reality of course is that that isn't who Satan is at all.

In the Bible, Satan is never presented as an object of fun, quite the contrary. He is very much a force to be reckoned with. He is the embodiment of all evil and the adversary of all good who seeks constantly to lure us from those truths that truly bring us peace and happiness. And demons are his servants, existing and active in us and among us.

In Biblical and many other cultures, demons are the cause of all sickness (mental and physical), the forces responsible for much of human sin (and human misery), and always opposed to God's purposes and God's people.

Whatever one may think of this in a scientifically-enlightened age, the truth that underlies it cannot be easily dismissed. One would have to be living on the moon not to admit that evil exists in our world and in us. Nor can one reasonably deny the destructive force of evil, both personal and global. And, while it is true that much of the misery in our world and our individual lives is caused by natural calamities and/or our own freely willed indifference and stupidity, much of it is also caused by forces within ourselves that entice us and drive us to where we do not want to go.

These are our "inner demons." They are those spiritual forces within us constantly whispering in our ears that our real happiness and peace will be found only when we listen to them and do what they suggest. Psychology and other therapeutic treatment can help us to identify the basis from which these forces operate and give us help in controlling them, but they are not the whole answer. In spite of the help these treatments can give, our demons are often too strong. We need added help if they are not to destroy us.

To effectively control our inner demons, we must be aware of the need to deal with them spiritually as well as physically and psychologically. They are of our spirit, as well as our flesh.

We no longer view demons as the cause of all illness, physical and mental, as people did in Biblical times. But if you doubt their continued existence, speak to the addict who knows well the destructive power of the addiction, who has come to loathe it and yet remains powerless to control it.

Whether or not one calls this inner person "the soul" is of little importance. The fact remains that total health and healing demands that we pay as much attention to our inner healing as we do to the outer. The psychosomatic and the somatic are undeniably intertwined.

This is why in dealing with our inner demons we must be aware of the need to deal with them spiritually as well as physically and psychologically. We cannot be "whole" without treating the whole person.

Even in Biblical times, demons were recognized as having power beyond their ability to cause illnesses. "It is by the power of Beelzebub, prince of devils, that he casts our demons," was how Jesus' opponents tried to explain away his good works.

This naming of the "prince of devils" (Beelzebub) was not accidental. Ancient people knew that control over their demons had to begin with naming them. The same is true for us.

Whatever their name: "Significant Other," "Fear," or

"Despair," our inner demons establish within us a strong inclination to that interior and destructive evil that can be called "sin."

I like to define sin as excessive self-loving, loving myself to such an excessive degree that I become the sole centre of my universe and no one else matters. What counts is what I want to have, what I want to do and my exclusive right to have and to do what I want.

This inordinate loving inescapably involves the breaking of those laws and Commandments that exist to regulate and protect healthy and life-giving love: that love, to which I am called, love of myself, of God and of neighbour.

The violation of laws, however, is not the essence of sin. That lies in distorted self-love that generates an inordinate and destructive need for absolute control over my life and perhaps the lives of those around me. In other words, the ultimate root of sin lies in an all-consuming and cold-hearted need/desire to be God.

This is the heart of that "first sin" recounted in the biblical story of Adam and Eve. It is true that their sin involves disobedience to God's command. But, it is more. It is a rupturing of the love God has shown them and the trust he has placed in them. And, what impels them to the sin is the whispered voice of the demon: "You will be gods." This is what they cannot resist. Sadly, while they see their actions as the ultimate road to their happiness, it is in fact the painful road to their loss. This is always the fallacy and the legacy of sin.

There is, then, validity in looking at our inner demons and their work from a spiritual as well as a psychological perspective. One does not need to contrive this link; it already exists and must be dealt with if the healing process is to be holistic and complete. If not for all of us, then for most of us, the voices of our inner demons are never totally silenced, never completely eradicated. The best we can hope to do is control them instead of being victims of their control. The grounding for this control is always found in true love. It is this love that is also the sole source of real virtue and all forms of health.

In Christian morality, this inordinate loving, which I call sin, finds its root expression in those seven human tendencies called the Capital Sins: lust, avarice, gluttony, envy, pride, anger (wrath) and sloth (acedia). Each of these is an embodiment of the real demon with which we must deal. Lust, Gluttony, Pride, along with their collaborators and offshoots, are the disguises through which inordinate love operates. And, no matter what other name or names these demons may use to try and deceive us, their real names will be found in the list of these seven.

From a spiritual point of view, any effective approach to effective inner healing must take them into account. Our most complete healing will come about when we name them and attack them directly, not through some alias they assume.

It will also demand an appropriate level of trust in ourselves, in the love of others and, above all, in God.

Chapter 3: Intimacy and Spirituality

"Live on in my love." (Jn 15, 9)

Trust in God requires at least a basic understanding of two essentials: "intimacy" and "spirituality."

We are all at least somewhat familiar with the meaning of the word intimacy. But what do we mean by spirituality?

The word "spirituality" refers to the set of values and principles that infuse one's life and give it direction. In non-religious or secular terms, spirituality is the quest to find the meaning of one's life and one's relationship to others and/or nature.

In religious terms, spirituality is also an attempt to answer some very basic questions: What does it mean to be "perfect?" What is it to be "holy?" When and how does one reach the perfection to which we apparently are called? – or, in relational terms: What is expected of us in our relationship with God, ourselves and others?

For some, the idea of an intimate relationship with God may seem somewhat strange at best and irreverent at worst. Yet some degree of intimacy with God is essential for a healthy and productive spirituality. All too frequently, however, the images of God handed on to us engender a relationship of fear not intimacy. I have dealt in depth with these fear-driven images in my book <u>Who Is This God You Pray To?</u> – but a brief treatment of two of these images may be of help here.

God the Terrible Tyrant is certainly a God to whom one can relate only in fear. This is a God who relentlessly demands that we "toe the line" at all costs, to whom compassion and understanding are foreign words, who will condemn us to eternal damnation without any remorse. At best, he is the "divine book-keeper" who resolutely demands that the books be balanced. At worst, he is the tyrant who will allow no fault or flaw, no sin, and no arguing with what is perceived to be his implacable and immutable will. One cannot be intimate with a tyrant: human or divine.

God the Mythical, Magical Force is likewise one with whom intimacy is impossible. This image robs God of all personality. It reduces Him to It. God simply becomes an indefinable and basically unknowable "something." This image of God should not be too closely equated with the "Higher Power" required by the Twelve Step programme of Alcoholics Anonymous. What is defined here is some nebulous, indefinable, incomprehensible and universal "force" as in "May the Force be with you" of Star Wars fame. It finds its counter-part in the indefinable and mysterious, the creating and sustaining force of New Age philosophy. This image of God may not engender fear, but it cannot form the basis of an intimate relationship either. It makes God much too unknowable.

These are but two examples of several false images of God that may have been instilled in many of us during our formative years. They can remain with us throughout our lives unless we change or abandon them. If they do so, they preclude any hope of an intimate relationship with God.

They also fly in the face of His self-truth that God has shown us. The God who has shown and continues to show himself to us is very much the Divine Lover. He is in fact the embodiment of genuine love. It is true that He may challenge, confront and even punish. He may even for a time allow evil to rule. He will do these things because these are genuine components of authentic loving. Love always seeks the good of the other. At times that will involve the challenge to grow, the need to confront, and the punishment from which we can learn. But God will also be the Lover whose love is unrestricted and whose forgiveness is both eternal and all-encompassing.

This authentic image of God is essential for any who want to grow in intimacy with him. Genuine intimacy demands genuine love with its call to growth and the support, confrontation and forgiveness that this call requires. Intimacy implies a comfortable familiarity with the other and this necessitates knowing as deeply as possible the other in the other's truth.

Baring some sort of direct revelation, getting to know God in His truth is not easy for us. This truth is almost always mediated to us through the people and the events that form our life experience and are part of our personal life history. What love is and involves can only be learned by being willing to risk loving. When our human experience of loving and being loved reflects love in its authenticity, we deepen our understanding of God and God's love for us. The inevitable fruit of this is the birth and growth of intimacy.

To be truly life giving, however, intimacy, first of all, demands total honesty, the whole and complete truth about one's self and the other. There can be no room for covering over weaknesses and faults and sin. Always seeing one's self and the other in glowing terms may lead somewhere, but it won't lead to genuine intimacy. Intimacy also needs an appropriate degree of emotionality. The fact that some people are unable or choose not to express openly their emotions need not be a problem as long as this is understood and respected by others in the relationship. Being afraid of one's emotions, however, can lead to serious and stultifying difficulties. Conversely, those who live or try to live solely on an emotional level will likewise encounter severe problems both internally and in their relationships.

The healthy approach to emotionality is to recognize both the value and the power of emotions. Emotions are powerful, human characteristics. One needs to learn how to exercise proper control over them so they do not become destructive, but contribute to one's overall good. Balance is the operative word here as it is in every other human undertaking.

Expressing one's emotions is always a delicate matter. One needs to learn how to do so appropriately. In all relationships, however, there is both room and need for the freedom to show one's feelings. To reject the other's right in this area or to receive a proper emotional response with coldness, indifference or anger can be death dealing. Too often addiction occurs because legitimate emotions have been denied appropriate expression. Suppressed and repressed, they fester internally. When the pain becomes unbearable, relief is sought in some self-destructive way: drugs, alcohol, inappropriate sexual behaviour, etc.

If expressing one's emotions in a human, inter-personal relationship is sometimes fear engendering, expressing them in a God-me relationship can be even more so. One's image of God is of vital importance here. One can only be emotionally free with God when one has come to see God in His truth, that is, as the embodiment of unrestricted love who loves us in our totality, warts and all. Intimacy with God will grow when I find the freedom to shout out my anger at Him, when I can cry out to Him my frustration, disillusionment, despair, loss of self, and know that I will not be rejected because I do so.

It is also important that we recognize that we are not born knowing how to use and control our emotions. Emotional freedom is a learned experience. This is particularly true in one's intimate relationship with God. If we are going to have a real relationship with God, we have to have emotionally intimate relationships with human beings. God doesn't want us to have a superficial relationship with Him. He wants us to have passionate intimacy with Him. We have to practice this in our human relationships. Anything that stands in the way or takes us away from building solid relationships with other humans will take us away from God. This is the heart of sin. And perhaps nowhere does sin wreck worse havoc than in one's relationship with one's self.

Building relationships also means building an awareness and acceptance of the self in all its totality: not condoning one's weakness and sin, but acknowledging them and working to improve. Establishing intimacy with someone else requires, first of all, that one becomes intimate with one's self.

The intimacy we have been examining is best expressed in English by the word "friendship." St. Augustine describes a friend as someone who knows all about you and loves you just the same - someone who knows you as you fully are and whose love is not diminished by your darker side. This is why friendship

20

has been described as the highest form of true love. It accepts; it invites; it challenges – always for the good of the other. When one can live trustingly in and out of true, in-depth friendship, one can love intimately and freely, and can welcome with peace the healing light of self-revelation.

Chapter 4: A Healing Friendship

"... and what does the Lord require of you
but to do justice, to love kindness and to
walk humbly with your God."
(Micah 6, 8)

The previous Chapter dealt in a general way with the definition of spirituality as an indispensable component of the "God-we" relationship. All religious systems give birth to some definition of spirituality. Traditional Christian spirituality has come out of either the classical Greek or Hebrew concept of perfection. Each of these naturally reflects the mentality, values and culture from which it arises. Both have their value and their deficiencies and neither is mutually exclusive.

The Greek ideal of perfection differs substantially from the Hebrew. It has no patience with imperfections and leaves no room for even a reasonable acceptance of them. It simply holds up the ideal and tells us that our holiness depends on how much and how well we reflect it in our everyday lives, how well we measure up. The problem is that so very often we don't measure up very well. And, our falling short can easily lead us into guilt, dejection and surrender. To be "perfect" is never to sin, an ideal rather beyond the reach of ordinary mortals like you and me.

This is not to say that the Greek ideal of perfection is without merit. It keeps our call to holiness and perfection very much in our view and constantly challenges us to get out of our mediocrity, our laziness and our all too frequent tendency to take the line of least resistance and settle for "what is good enough."

But, for all its possible value, the Greek ideal of perfection is austere. It tends to create a distance between ourselves and God. It also lacks the acceptance and valuing of our humanness, which we find in the Hebrew tradition. And since much of what we will be talking about here deals with the healing of our human addictions and imperfections, it is important that we know that, in order to move towards this, we do not have to leave our humanness behind. We do not have to achieve perfect healing in order for God (and others) to love us and grace us with that love.

The Greek concept of spirituality can also cloud a basic truth of Christianity. Properly understood, the great gift of our redemption neither implies, nor demands, that we suddenly and miraculously cease to be a sinner. We are and remain sinners. What redemption can and should bring us is the firm assurance that now we are loved sinners. In the light and hope of that knowledge we can deal, albeit imperfectly, with the demonic voices within us that are constantly trying to convince us that for us there is no hope.

Recognition of this truth is one of the strengths of the Hebrew concept both of redemption and of our struggle to incarnate the redemptive process in our lives. The Hebrew approach to union with God does not demand that we rid ourselves of all our weaknesses, flaws and sin. Quite the contrary. It does not see our humanness as an obstacle to our union with God but rather as our need for union with God.

In contrast, the Greek model of perfection sees us as subservient partners in the God-us union. It is as if we were, for example, a block of marble at which God chisels away until the perfect statue emerges. Our role chiefly consists in an openness and willingness to allow God to rid the marble of all imperfections. In so doing, we both aid and make possible the perfect image God wants to sculpt. This God-us relationship, into which Greek spirituality calls us, is characterized more accurately as a parent-child or master-pupil relationship than by the friend-to-friend relationship that forms the heart of the Hebrew concept. And because of this emphasis, it is the Hebrew spirituality that will serve us best as we wrestle with our inner demons and their destructiveness.

The Hebrew Scriptures provide lots of examples of this friendship bond between God and the people with whom he interacts. I want to cite two: the bargaining between God and Abraham over God's proposed destruction of Sodom and Gomorrah, and Moses' venting of his frustration and anger at God over the leadership task God has given him.

First, Abraham to God:

> Then Abraham came near and said, "Will you indeed sweep away the innocent with the wicked? Suppose there are fifty innocent people within the city; will you wipe out the place and not forgive it for the fifty innocent people who are in it? Far be it from you to do such a thing, to make the innocent die with the wicked, so that the innocent and the guilty should be treated alike. Should not the judge of the world act with justice?" The Lord replied, "If I find fifty innocent people in the city of Sodom, I will spare the whole place for their sake."
>
> Abraham spoke up again: "See how I am presuming to speak to my Lord, though I am but dust and ashes! What if there are five less than fifty innocent people? Will you destroy the whole city because of those

five?" "I will not destroy it," he answered, if I find forty-five there." But Abraham persisted, saying, "What if only forty are found there?" The Lord replied, "I will forbear doing it for the sake of forty." Then Abraham said, "Let not my Lord grow impatient if I go on. What if only thirty are found there?" God replied, "I will forbear doing it if I find only thirty there." Still Abraham went on, "Since I have dared to speak to my Lord, what if there are no more than twenty?" "I will not destroy it, he answered. I will spare it for the sake of the twenty." But Abraham still persisted, "Please, let not my Lord grow angry if I speak up one last time. What if there are at least ten there?" The Lord replied, "For the sake of those ten, I will not destroy the city." The Lord departed as soon as he had finished speaking with Abraham and Abraham returned home. (Genesis 18, 22 – 23)

Now, Moses to God:

When Moses heard the people, family after family, crying at the entrance of their tents, so that the Lord became very angry, he was grieved. "Why do you treat your servant so badly?" Moses asked the Lord. "Why are you so displeased with me that you burden me with all this people? Was it I who conceived all this people? Or was it I who gave them birth, that you tell me to carry

them at my bosom like a foster father carrying an infant to a land you have promised under oath to their fathers? Where can I find meat to give to all this people? For they are crying to me, 'Give us meat for our food.' I cannot carry all this people by myself, for they are too heavy for me. If this is the way you will deal with me, then please do me the favour of killing me at once so that I need no longer face this distress."
(Numbers 11, 10 – 15)

Several additional examples could be cited. They are all characterized by the trust, respect and easy interplay that mark true friendship.

A more modern, non-Scriptural example would be Tevye, the lead character in the play Fiddler on the Roof. So much of his prayer reflects this friendship aspect that it is perhaps unfair to single out any one line or scene. But, the one that stays so prominently with me is the scene where he wants to lament his poverty, but doesn't want to offend God by doing so. He resolves his dilemma by saying: "God, I know you love the poor, but couldn't you love me a little less?" It is a line filled with respect for God's role in his life and in the universe and, at the same time, filled with that familiarity and playfulness born of a genuine friendship.

This element of friendship in the Hebrew ideal of perfection has another very important aspect: it frees us to approach God and to enter into meaningful relationship with him at any given stage of our life. We do not have to be "perfect" in order to be with God. In the Hebrew tradition, God asks us to become perfect, not in any abstract or impossible way, but by being the best person we can be in all our relationships. What is important is not ridding ourselves of all the flaws and imperfections of our humanness, but controlling and striving to overcome these so that we can truly become persons of justice, compassion, charity and forgiveness. The psalms often echo this theme and it finds a very strong expression in this passage from the prophet Micah: "You have been told, O mortal, what is good; and what does the Lord require of you but to do justice, and to love kindness and to walk humbly, with your God?" (Micah 6, 8)

There is a great validity in the Hebrew approach to relationships whether with God or other human beings. Instead of our weaknesses being a problem, they can become for us, and for others, a real source of ministry. Those who acknowledge honestly their own weaknesses and sin are by far the best ministers to the weaknesses and sins of others. And, since all inner healing begins with acknowledging the truth, they are also the best ministers to themselves.

As effective as the Greek approach to holiness may be, for most of us it is the Hebrew model with its call to healing intimacy with God and ourselves that allows us to deal most effectively with our inner demons. Inner healing requires the freedom to speak our truth to a loving other. It is about the freedom to open our hearts and softening the places that won't let love in. In the process we call healing, we rock back and forth between the abuse of the past and the fullness of the present. It is this rocking that creates the healing.

The purpose of healing is not to be happy forever, to

once and for all rid ourselves of the pain and the struggle. This is not possible. The inner demons do not give up. They do not leave us alone. They never go away. What healing does do is allow us to regain control. It is about being awake to the powers that would destroy us and learning how to control them at least most of the time. It is about being alert and awake so that we are not taken off guard. It is about being broken and whole at the same time. It is learning to live while we are alive instead of enduring a living death. It is learning that we can be and are loved in the totality of our personhood, that we do not have to exist in the perfection that others may demand of us. For that, we need a true friend, someone who does know all about us and loves us just the same. It is in the love of a true friend that we can touch God's love for us and find the happiness God wills for us. Only love gives life in its fullness.

PART II: THE DEMONS

Chapter 5: Naming the Demons

"Only the Holy Spirit can purify the mind . . . So by every means, but especially by peace of soul, we must try to provide the Spirit with a resting place. Then we shall have the light of knowledge shining within us at all times, and it will show up for what they are: all the hateful temptations that come from demons, and not only will it show them up: their exposure will also greatly diminish their power." (Diadochus of Photice, bishop)

"Of all the many wondrous things, nothing is more wondrous than man," so sings the chorus in the play Antigone, written centuries ago by the great Greek tragedian, Sophocles.

Nothing has changed us over the centuries. We are still a wondrous mixture of good and evil, wholeness and brokenness, dreams and nightmares. Behind our smiles often lurks suffering. Our laughter often hides our pain.

And the dark propensities within us still underlie all human tragedy in literature and in life. We all carry within us some Achilles' heel, some fatal flaw, some demonic voice or voices pushing us so that the dilemma which St. Paul expresses with such anguish is also ours. "The good I want to do I do not do and the evil I do not want to do, I do." (Rm 7, 21) When this happens, our demons are at work.

If we want to deal with our demons in a healing way, we must first name them. We cannot deal with what we refuse to acknowledge. That is why demonic healing in the gospels always begins with a dialogue around the name of the demon. And like the demon in the following gospel passage the demon's name often is "legion," not necessarily because one of us is possessed by more than one demon but because the demon is so good at disguise. "What is your name," we cry. And the demon answers: "alcoholism" or "drugs" or "sexual addiction." But all good therapy, psychological and spiritual, sees through the disguise and realizes that worthwhile healing cannot stop there. What has to be found is the demon's real name. And the real name of the demon truly is Legion.

They came to the other side of the sea, to the country of the Gerasenes. And when he had stepped out of the boat, he was immediately met by a man from the tombs who had an unclean spirit . . . "What is your name?" Jesus asked him. He replied: "My name is Legion; for we are many." (Mk. 5, 1-2; 9)

Chapter 6: "Significant Other"

"We are in a sense our own parents and we give birth to ourselves by our own choices."
(Gregory of Nyssa)

That term "significant other" is so common today that I wonder if we really appreciate its impact. Do we ever fully understand just how significant our significant others really are? Those who deal therapeutically with the victims of addiction know well the damage inflicted by dysfunctional parent-child relationships. Since our parents are, or were, no more perfect than we, all of us suffer to some extent from this type of relationship. For many of us the damage is relatively minor and is relatively easy to deal with as we mature. We may even be able to use our damaged areas as strengths to contribute to our growth as persons.

A good many others live from a different scenario. For them the damage not only lasts, it also sets up within them a constant battle between the demands and expectations of their parents and those that are their own. This is true even if the parents are no longer alive. The parental demands may be so integrated in their sense of self that it is as if the parent(s) is still living. Almost always their own identity has to be denied in favour of who their parents demand they must be.

In the vital areas of sexuality and personality they are thus robbed of the freedom to develop in the truth of the person they really are. Homosexual orientation must be hidden at all costs. Failure is never tolerated, let alone accepted with love, understanding and forgiveness. One must strive even to the point of self-destruction if necessary in order to fulfill the parental ambitions placed on the child – ambitions spelled out very clearly and all too commonly overlaid with the threat of rejection, implicitly or strongly conveyed.

Enter the demon of deceit, of pretence, of living in

the angry world of constant lying: lying certainly to others and very often to oneself as well. This demon leads its victim into the world of "the closet." This is the world into which no mirror can be introduced. There is too great a risk that what will be mirrored will be the real me and not the carefully constructed façade I have so meticulously built in the interests of self-preservation.

The suffering and the self-destruction involved here is unimaginable to any who have never experienced it. And in too many cases, the façade, the mask, the pretence, is only sustainable through excessive use of alcohol or drugs or destructive sexual activity or anything else that enables one to escape or to endure the pain of the reality in which the sufferer lives.

And while it is true that many of us are able to work our way out of domination by destructive/dysfunctional parent-child relationships, it is equally true that the scars remain. We may win the battle but the struggle can last a lifetime. Many others simply lose the fight itself and go on living their lives in varying degrees of despair and desperation. Even those who have won the battle often remain fearful that it is just that battle they have won, that there will be other battles that they will lose. They fear that, in the long run, their losses will greatly out-number the victories. The final victor will be total defeat.

I have been speaking of biological parents. All of us, however, have other "parental" relationships. These relationships often reinforce response patterns planted in us by abusive, dysfunctional, destructive relationships with our biological parents. Lovers as well as bosses and others in authority over us can take the place of birth parents. Traumatic events in life also can, and often do, assume a persona of their own and damage their victims. The following life-story witnesses the destructive control that can be brought to bear by a significant other.

"I have spent my life struggling with the damage done to me by significant others. The dominant person in my parent-child relationship was my mother. Physically, she died many years ago. In actuality, she has continued to live in me. I still have to deal with her demands and expectations: never fail; do everything perfectly, succeed at all costs to yourself and others.

I still feel her rejection when I do fail or do not do a "perfect" job. Sometimes I still live out of the fundamental fact of our relationship: that I will never be loved for who I am, but only for what I can do, accomplish, achieve. In many ways I still live in fear of her and her power over me. There are times when she robs me of my power even now.

There are still times when I operate out of a need to please and the fear of rejection if I should fail to do so. And, try as I might to shut my mother out of my life and close the door on her, she usually finds a way back in.

In adulthood, I simply transferred my mother's voice to the authority figures in my life. They possessed all of her power over me. Above all, I was convinced that I had to constantly and consistently please them – or suffer the consequent rejection.

I never felt valued for my self, but only for what I could do. I often wondered if my mother wanted to give me birth or if I was an unwanted "accident." Nothing was ever said but the vibes were strong.

The result of all this is that I was very open to manipulation and control by others in my life. As it inevitably does, all this led to pain and, in the long run, destruction. In my eyes, my self-value was nil.

The most damaging effect of this conditioning centered on love. I never felt that anyone loved me for myself. Like my mother, everyone loved me solely for what I could do. And "everyone" included God.

Intellectually, I could accept the truth of God's unrestricted love for me. Emotionally, I could not. God was my mother incarnate. The price for not being rejected by him was the same.

I had no real friends. How could I have had? True friendship can only develop when two people meet on their deepest levels, in the openness of honest self-revelation. I could never do that. The real "me" had to be hidden. It might not please. What I presented to others was a well-constructed, hollow image of myself, carefully tailored to avoid rejection.

Inevitably, the crash came, as it had to come. Its result was total burn out: physical, emotional, spiritual. I had no strength to do anything. That was horribly frightening. Nobody loved me for myself. Everyone {God included} only "loved" me for what I could do. Since I could now do nothing, who would love me? Did I any longer have any self worth? I entered the living death of despair and despondency.

Yet, in the midst of all the pain and darkness, I somehow knew that what I was experiencing was a grace. That, in some way, the God I barely knew was leading me. There would be a way out of the darkness. The pain would be a healing pain.

My path out of this darkness was lit by two people who gradually became close friends. Throughout this terrible ordeal their love for me was constant and gave me new sight. I came to the realization that their love could not have been based on what I could do since, at that time, I could do nothing. Their love had to be directed to me as person, not as achiever. It must have been difficult for them at times. I challenged and rejected them. I suspected their motivation. Gratefully, they persevered. Many times the love they showed me was "tough love." They challenged and confronted, sometimes very strongly.

Finally their efforts bore fruit. I began to realize that if these two loved me even though I could *do* nothing, then they really did love *me*.

The realization of my innate loveability was their gift to me. My immediate healing flowed from that. Later in life, I would have to deal with the residue of the rage left in me by my previous life experiences, but eventually my healing came and I no longer see myself in that destructive light."

I wanted to deal first with this name for Legion ("Significant Other") because it is so often the foundation out of which so much dysfunctional behaviour and so many destructive addictions flow. It also gives birth to two other foundational names that need to be dealt with here. The first of these is "Fear."

Chapter 7: "Fear"

"Do not let your hearts be troubled . . . trust in me." (Jn 14, 1)

Fear paralyzes. The fear I'm talking about anyway. Its power is enormous. Its effects are devastating. So many things, we dare not attempt. So much of us, we dare not reveal. So many scars are left by the significant others in our past life. So much darkness, pain, despair. "Climb every mountain" the song urges. But there are mountains deep in the darkness of our souls that we dare not climb and dare not expose to the healing light of love. We are fearful that there is no healing light of love. Worse still is the fear that if there is such a light, it will only reveal how unworthy we are to receive its gift. To avoid exposing what we fear to expose we spend our energy maintaining the darkness even when the light desperately wants to penetrate the cracks in our armour.

And so we stay in our "what should we do?/ what can we do state?" filled with anxiety and self-loathing, fearing above all that someone else may light up the darkness we expend so much energy to maintain. "Fear not," Jesus says. How can we not fear when this fear is so powerful, when this demon seems to be so strong, when even Jesus seems unable to drive it out of us?

And this demon itself has so many sub-names. Perhaps the worst of these is: "fear of self-revelation." No one must ever be allowed to know the real us: our innermost thoughts, desires, sexuality – all the subterranean material that, in the darkness of our tomb, the demon of fear feeds on and on and on. And he has great allies this demon, related tormentors that nourish and strengthen the paralyzing fear that rules us: the fear of rejection, of failure, of loss of "image." So every morning we put on the mask and get ready to face the day in fear and trembling, never quite sure how others will react should the mask be ripped from our face and our true self exposed, unaware of the exact nature and name of the demon(s) driving us.

Each of these demons has its own voice. "Fear of Rejection" whispers strongly in our ear: "Hide or suffer the disdain, the revulsion, perhaps even the hatred that will certainly come if you let the truth be known." At the same time "Fear of Failure" whispers: "You must not fail; you cannot afford to fail. Drive yourself mercilessly to succeed. Use those around you as props and demand perfection of them lest they make you look bad. Cheat. Lie. Manipulate. Do whatever you have to do in order to succeed or suffer the consequences. They do not love you. They only love what you can do! You have to prove that you are good for something or die trying. The 'image' has to be kept at all costs. The consequences of its loss are simply too destructive." And in our fear, we agree. And in agreeing, we die a little each day.

These are the voices our Significant Others have programmed on our inner tape recorder. We hear them strongly and with great anxiety. The tape runs continuously, triggered by this or that. In the pain of being unloved, we look for alleviation in work, sex, drugs, alcohol. In desperation, we cling to anything and anyone that gives us rest from the pain, that creates the illusion that really things aren't so bad after all. In the pain of feeling unlovable, we do the very things that will increase our shame and guarantee our unlovability.

Eventually these anesthetics become indispensable "friends." Although they don't exorcise the fear-inducing demon(s), they do enable us to cope with the indescribable pain. With them we can function

47

sufficiently enough to don the mask and live the image at least for another day.

In the end, however, our "indispensable friends" can no longer sustain us in living our illusion. The victory goes to the demon Fear and his allies. And we lie broken amid the shattered ruins of our carefully constructed image. Falsely, we come to believe that, for us, there is no hope. We want to be wrong. We want to believe in our innate goodness and beauty and value. We want to walk in hope. We want to run to the light, the healing light of our truth. We cannot. We are too afraid. We cannot risk. So we remain enslaved by Fear.

I have known this demon "Fear" all my life. Its dominion over me has become less severe, but not erased. My conditioning at the hands of the significant others in my past is still influencing me. I still fear not being "perfect." I still fear failure and rejection. I am still wary of even legitimate self-revelation. Fear may not paralyze me as it used to, but even now it can cause me to fret, worry and sweat over tasks, even over those I know I can accomplish with relative ease. I must always be vigilant. If I allow my coping mechanisms to slip, Fear once again paralyzes me.

Whenever I find myself beginning to slip, I run to that Light, which is Jesus. This image of light is essential. Growth takes place only in light. God's presence in our lives is manifested in terms of light. His care and concern for his people is imaged by light. Followers of Buddha speak of the journey to enlightenment as the heart of their spiritual quest. The pillar of fire guided the Hebrews to safety as they fled their slavery in Egypt. The Koran states that: "God is the light of heaven and earth," and "God will direct unto his light those whom he pleases." (Chapter 24)

For Christians, it is Jesus who is "the Light of the world." Jesus used this designation himself. John reiterates it in his gospel account. Referring to Jesus, John writes: "What has come into being in him was life, and the life was the light of all people. The light shines in the darkness, and the darkness does not overcome it." (Jn 1, 4 – 5)

Healing begins when we find the courage to take our first halting steps into the light. Demons thrive only in the dark. The more they are exposed to light, the less powerful they are. In total darkness we see only black. In the semi-darkness we can discern shapes and forms. Often these are distortions that we mistake for realities. In both situations, the demons can easily lead us with their lies. Only in the strength of full light, can we see the truth. Only in seeing and accepting the whole truth of our personhood can we find life.

That is why John intimately connects light and life. In the person of Jesus, the incarnated God, Light and Life co-exist. The Light who is Jesus shines in our darkness and illumines the truth of God's love for us at every stage of our existence. In that truth we can come to know both our need for love and our lovability. We can truthfully and fearlessly acknowledge the fullness of our reality. We can face without fear both the tendency to evil and the goodness and beauty that co-exist in all of us. This is the truth that sets us free. (Jn 8, 32)

Convincing ourselves that God loves us can be difficult. Talking about God's unconditional love is easy. Being convinced of it is much more difficult. God may indeed know our whole truth and love us just the same.

Knowing that, however, will not free one from the fear of rejection. To be effective, God's love has to be experienced. Only then will it become a conviction out of which one can live.

It will take time for that conviction to grow. The love of others will strengthen it. Others' rejection will weaken, even destroy it. Our first steps into the light will be hesitant and faltering. The process will usually be crab-like: advance-retreat, one step forward, two steps back. We zigzag between the goodness we want to be and the evil we see ourselves to be.

In a very real way, we are all replicas of the Prodigal Son: of his ingratitude, his callousness, his lust. (Lk 15, 11 - 32) We share the shame of the woman taken in adultery. (Jn 8) We utter the forlorn cry of the lost sheep. (Lk 15, 3 - 7) These are our experiences too. They possess us, overwhelm us. They tell us how awful we are. They reinforce our sense of rejection. We cannot move beyond our self-loathing. We see only our guilt. There is no beauty in us. Love is an impossible dream.

Invariably the real message eludes us: the message that is the whole point of these Biblical events, the message that is in God's voice: "I will never abandon you; I yearn for you; I seek you; I call you back to my arms." God's voice shouts forgiveness, acceptance of us and exhilarating joy at our struggle to return. God waits for us, not with disapproving anger, but with a bear hug and radiant smile.

We cannot receive the message in the abstract. We will only hear it when we see the same smile on another's face, when another's arms reach us, not to push us away, but to hug us, to hold us close, to let us hear a heart beating with love for us as we are in that moment. When this happens, we can begin to become whole.

This is the seedbed of the conviction that God loves us unconditionally – a conviction born in the unconditional love of another human being. It is the fruit of our freedom to say to another: "This is my dark side" and to hear in reply: "None of that is a problem for me."

But even when we experience that love we can still be on shaky ground. Our experiences all too often teach us the inconstancy, the fickleness of human love. Instinctively we search for a love that is constant and eternal: a love that will never be conditional. One in which our acceptance is eternally secure. A love that resides only in God.

The door to that love is always open to us. We have only to enter it. We need only to become convinced of its existence, its reality and its truth. We will always be God's Beloved. In God's eyes our lovability is never in question. If we become convinced of that truth nothing will be able to destroy us. The slings and arrows others may throw at us will never pierce our hearts.

St. Paul speaks from this conviction when he writes: "If God is for us, who is against us? He who did not withhold his own Son, but gave him up for all of us, will he not with him also give us everything else? - Who will separate us from the love of Christ? Will hardship, or distress, or persecution, or famine, or nakedness, or peril, or sword? – No, in all these things we are more than conquerors through him who loved us. For I am convinced that neither death, nor life, nor angels, nor rulers, nor things past or present, nor things to come, nor powers, nor height, nor depth, nor anything else in all creation, will be able to separate us from the love of God in Christ Jesus our Lord." (Rm, 8, 31-39)

In the rejection that plagued his life, Paul grew in his conviction of the Father's love for him. In the strength of that love he found the freedom to be all who he was. The same path can be ours as well. Our peace will come when we find the courage to follow it.

The path will not be easy. Obstacles will abound. Progress will be erratic and slow. But, with patience and determination, we will arrive. Upon arriving, we will enter the Light of Love. And, upon entering, we will find hope and life.

"As important as your past is, because it got you where you are, it is not nearly as important as how you see your future. If there is faith in the future, there is power in the present." (Zig Zigleir)

Chapter 8: "Despair"

"Abandon hope all you who enter here."
(Dante: The Divine Comedy)

"Despair" is the child of the demons "Significant Others" and "Fear." It is the most destructive of all the demons. It calls for the abandonment of all faith, all hope. It is used with great effectiveness by those who would destroy or exercise diabolic control over others in countries, concentration camps, prisons - in any living hell. And, in the spiritual realm it is Evil's ultimate weapon.

Faith and hope are essential in maintaining one's life-giving sense of personal dignity, one's self-value and freedom. Destroy those and the victim becomes an object, open to whatever use and abuse the manipulator wants to inflict.

To maintain a healthy control over our lives, we must have faith in that Higher Power some call God. We must also have faith in ourselves and in others with whom we interact.

Faith and hope always go together. If we live in faith, we also live in hope. In this living we then discover love, the source and the nurturer of both faith and hope.

The demon called "Despair" knows all this only too well. To reach his goal, he must destroy faith and hope. Once that is done, the destruction of the person is inevitable. The person becomes dehumanized, reduced to the status of a "thing."

When we look around and see only darkness, when we collapse exhausted in defeat, when we have exerted so much and such constant effort in achieving little or nothing, these are the times "Despair" whispers so strongly: "What is the use? You can't win so why keep up the struggle? Just give up and give in; that's where your peace, your happiness or at least your relief truly lies."

If we listen to Despair's voice, in spite of all our efforts, we remain slaves to whatever addiction or sinful habits plague us. We grow angry at the demon who controls us. We come to hate him and to hate ourselves for being his slave. In desperation we double our efforts to be free. But nothing seems to work. We always end up in defeat.

Eventually we become worn out by the constant and futile struggle. We long for rest. We find none. We want to regain control of our lives. The prospect of doing that overwhelms us with Fear. We want to get rid of the mask. Yet we hear too strongly our Significant Other's voice saying: "You need the mask. As flawed as you are, you will never be accepted." And this Significant Other finds support in the Greek model of spirituality with its stress on perfection (as outlined in chapter 4.)

Fear of failure then drives us to succeed. We become convinced that we do not have what it takes. Inevitably we turn to anything that will dull the pain, that will help us keep up our image and enable us to go on. Anything will do as long as it props us up and give us the courage to face and deal with another day.

Eventually these props become indispensable "friends." They don't rid us of "Despair." They are simply crutches enabling us to cope with the often-indescribable pain. They let us don the mask and live the image at least for one more hour, one more day.

In the end these "friends" can no longer sustain my self-delusion. The demon wins and I lie broken and shattered among the ruins of my self-worth and my carefully constructed image.

Before we reach the state of total despair somewhere deep inside us another voice whispers that the demon's words are only a diabolical trap. But unless we can find the resources to strengthen this deeper voice, it becomes fainter and fainter until it is over-powered by the demon. We then abandon all hope and enter our ultimate hell.

The saving truth is that the demon in us is a liar, as cunning and clever a liar as the demon who tempted Adam and Eve. "Despair" does not need to win. We may have to live with our past. We do not have to live out of it. Nothing has to rule and run us forever. The truth is that there is always hope. This is the truth that "Despair" does not want us ever to know.

Maybe hope will be born and nurtured by the concern, care and strengthening of those who truly love us. Perhaps it will be born of some drastic event that forces us to choose between life and death, self-loving and self-destroying. Maybe it will be the gift of some glimmer of faith, no matter how weak, that helps us cling to the truth of God's unreserved love for us. With this faith we will be enabled to know the equally valid truth that every "death" leads only to life-giving resurrection.

In the last analysis, love unfailingly conquers all things. If I remain open to the love of God and others, as difficult as that may prove to be, the whispering voice reinforcing my self-worth, my value, my uniqueness will grow increasingly stronger. And the demon "Despair" will be bound at last.

Chapter 9: Lust

Lust takes no thought of consequences; the thrill of a particular challenge or of immediate satisfaction dominate relationship and action.
(The Seven Deadly Sins;
p. 138 Upper Room Books)

Someone once said that all of us have a favourite sin. If a poll were taken, Lust would rank high.

There can be no reasonable denial of the power of the demon we call Lust or, for that matter, any of the other of its allied demons operating under the names of the other capital sins. They can all rule us and destroy us. They are all-pervasive.

Lust, especially, has great power. There are other sources of its power but in part it is due to the fact that Lust is so endemic to human nature. It is so much a part of our common darker side, so opposed to that purity of mind and action to which our spiritual side calls us.

The very word "purity" is indicative of a central problem in our treatment of Lust because it reflects our common and all too restrictive understanding of Lust. It leads us to think of Lust exclusively in terms of sexual activity.

In reality, Lust's range of activity is much broader. It also covers the strong and unreasonable push many have for power, money, position, fame, etc. In all these areas, as well as in the sexual, our motives can be "impure." Even so, unfortunately we still tend to see purity solely in terms of sexual purity. We also tend to draw an exclusive equal sign between Lust and sex.

In doing so, we sell Lust short. We minimize his scope. We fail to recognize his power and his influence in other equally vulnerable areas of our human psyche. We see sex as his sole alias and so we forget that he has others.

Lust is so powerful, partly because he hides behind half-truths. He can whisper in our ear that there is nothing wrong with having sex or pursuing fame and fortune and he is right. What he fails to tell us is that the unbridled pursuit of these things is highly destructive. Though they are natural and good in their proper use, they become agents of addiction when they get out of hand. And Lust will inevitably push us over the edge unless we make every reasonable effort to contain him.

Trying to contain Lust brings to the fore the second source of his great power: he is terribly, powerfully persistent.

This persistence, combined with the half-truths he hides behind, makes Lust seem undefeatable. Once he has us firmly in his grip, our struggles to break free seem futile. It's like wrestling with a boa constrictor. The more we struggle, the tighter the grip becomes until gradually the fight is squeezed out of us. We then become the exhausted victim, immobile in the power of our captor. Escape from its clutches seems totally hopeless.

It is at this point that Lust unites forces with that other demon, Despair. And Despair finalizes our defeat. Any shred of hope we may have clung to is snatched away. We live now in a state of hopelessness. Seeing no way to escape Lust's grasp we surrender to his control and become his victim.

In our surrender, we discover Lust's real name. It is "control" – not control of, but control over, with its synonyms domination and victimization.

It is this demonic name, Control, that Paul identifies so clearly in chapter seven of his Letter to the Romans: " . . . but I am of the flesh, sold into slavery under sin . . . I do not understand my own actions. For I do not do what I want, but I do the very thing I hate . . . For I do not do the good I want; but the evil I do not want is what

I do . . . making me a prisoner of the evil that dwells in my body."

We all know the truth of those words. And those who are suffering some strong addiction know it even better. The destructive force within us is a powerful force indeed. Whether we lust after sex or power or money or position, the demon will drive us, even to the brink of self-destruction. The struggle to wrest control from the demon can literally be one of life or death.

Lust pushes us continually to do what we do not want to do and to be where we do not want to be, physically, psychologically, spiritually. We become its slaves, chained to it, convinced by it that nothing we can do will free us. It convinces us that unless we fulfill its demands, we will know no peace, no joy.

Eventually we become aware that fulfilling Lust's demands can destroy us. At the same time we are afraid of the consequences if we refuse. Fear now joins Despair as Lust's helpmate. In the face of that three-fold power, we lie shattered and, all too often, filled with the poison of our own self-loathing.

Our social environment lends additional power to the three-fold attack by Lust, Despair and Fear. For many of us, our society adopts the voice of our Significant Others. Like these, society does not accept and has no healing patience with our failures and our flaws. Its ruling god is Success. Its central doctrine is that happiness lies in the all-consuming worship and service of that god. How this is to be done is of no importance as long as he is satisfied.

Lust also serves that god. He provides and enforces success's basic commandment: "There must be no restraints on your efforts to succeed. Use whatever you need: sex, lies, cheating, defamation of others, alcohol, drugs – whatever. Liberate yourself from all restrictions, moral and otherwise. Drive yourself. Use whatever you need to prop yourself up. The only thing that counts is success. True happiness lies only there."

These are not new words, new urgings. Humankind has heard them before. In essence, they were the words the Serpent whispered to Adam and Eve. They carry the same promise. They still bring the same destruction. They are the same lie. As in the case of Adam and Eve, the freedom these words promise eventually turns into chains. Those who listen, and accept them as true, end up caught more and more securely in Lust's net.

The fallacy of Lust's words gradually surfaces. Deep within us we know that enduring, soul-depth happiness is not found in living Lust's lie. It is found instead in whatever pain may come in resisting it. Self-destruction is never the road to peace and fulfillment.

But the ropes of Lust's net are strong. The desires he fosters tempt and entice us. Even the illusion of success and happiness and peace is better than nothing at all. We become much too afraid to let go of our "friends." We increasingly need and depend on their support in our quest.

In reality, no addiction brings us happiness. It only brings pain. Lust's call to us to "liberate" ourselves, sexually and otherwise, will eventually imprison us ever more devastatingly.

Only in genuinely loving and finding authentic love will we be able to walk the path out of Lust's darkness into the light of our true freedom. In the love other's have for us, we fulfill our basic need for self-acceptance and self-valuing. In our love for others, we fulfill these essential needs in them. Destroying Lust's hold will only be accomplished through growth in genuine self-love. For many of us, this is the most difficult task of all. And living out of Lust doesn't make it any easier.

In fact, Lust destroys love. It is so filled with self-seeking that it leaves no room for self-giving. It says loud and clear to the beloved: "I will 'love' you as long as you meet my needs. Don't expect me to try too hard to meet yours. And when I decide that you no longer meet my needs I will leave you and find someone else who does."

This "love" imprisons the other. The beloved has no choice but to live within the prison of the "lover's" expectations and demands. If he or she needs the other to be thin, the other cannot be fat; if the need is for the other to be blond, he or she cannot be brunette and so on.

This form of "love" is called "erotic love" because it seeks only its own pleasure, its own happiness. And it imprisons because it forces the beloved to live continually in some ugly time warp, fearful of any change. The loved one cannot grow, cannot change because the risk is too great. The change may not meet the other's current "need" and the penalty for that has been made all too clear.

Hopefully, at some point we will understand that to live we must break the death grip Lust has on us. Breaking that hold will require the help of a true friend. One who will tell us the truth about ourselves: our goodness, our beauty, our worth. One who is not put off by our past mistakes. One who knowing our weaknesses and sin, loves us just the same. One whose love can convince us that, for us, as for that other Prodigal Son, it is never too late to come to our senses. That, like him, we too have a Father who, in his unreserved love for us, constantly searches for us and hopes for our return. That we, too, can always go home.

When the light comes near us, especially that Light we call our God, then like Adam and Eve we see ourselves in our nakedness and, terrified, we want to hide. The Light shines too painfully. We cannot bear its truth and healing pain. So we retreat further and further into the darkness, into the grasp of the demon that dwells there, until finally we retreat too far. The darkness engulfs us totally and all hope of freeing ourselves seems lost.

At all costs we must resist the urge to hide. Lust is so powerful because its power is rooted deep in our basic need for self-acceptance and self-valuing, the essential elements of our self-loving. Exorcizing the demon called Lust will only be accomplished through growth in, what is for many, the most difficult of all tasks: genuine self-love.

Chapter 10: Avarice and Gluttony

"And [Jesus] said to them, "Take care! Be on your guard against all kinds of greed; for one's life does not consist in the abundance of possessions."
(Lk. 12, 15)

I am treating Avarice and Gluttony together for two reasons: they are opposite sides of the same coin, and, like many of the other deadly sins, they are both closely allied to Lust. All three push us unreasonably to destructive acquisition. In fact, sometimes it is difficult to tell precisely which of these three is doing the pushing. They are all geared to getting what we want and all we want with no regard to the damage done to ourselves or others.

Our society reinforces the power of this demonic trio. We are constantly being urged to seek "the perfect": the perfect body, the perfect environment, the perfect relationship, perfect health, perfect happiness, perfect everything.

We are not only urged to seek "the perfect," we are conditioned to believe that we have an inalienable right to get it and to hold on to it.

The modern mantras of media advertising all carry the same message: anything goes if it gets us what we want or where we want to be. The adverse and harmful consequences of our actions are never our responsibility. They are simply the results of our upbringing or our socioeconomic condition, of government or some other social agency. If nothing else excuses, we can always pass them off as simply the offshoots of our presumed and absolute right to get and to hold whatever is held out to us as "happiness" or "self-fulfillment."

In this "the-devil-made-me-do-it" attitude, we echo the self-excusing words of Adam and Eve when God confronted them after they had sinned:

> They heard the sound of the Lord walking in
> the garden at the time of the evening breeze,

and the man and his wife hid themselves from the presence of the Lord God among the trees of the garden. But the Lord God called to the man, and said to him, "Where were you?"

He said, "I heard the sound of you in the garden, and I was afraid, because I was naked; and I hid myself."

He said, "Who told you that you were naked? Have you eaten from the tree of which I commanded you not to eat?"

The man said, "The woman whom you gave to be with me, she gave me fruit from the tree, and I ate."

Then the Lord God said to the woman, "What is this that you have done?"

The woman said, "The serpent tricked me, and I ate."(Gen. 3, 8 -13)

This shifting of responsibility for our actions is very difficult to counter-attack. It speaks to our instinct to exercise our rights and avoid the corresponding obligations. It also caters to our strong desire to assume total control over our lives in an unhealthy and unloving way. In doing so, it draws its strength from our natural greed and our lust for power, comfort, acceptance and so forth.

Avarice, Gluttony and Lust all plug into this greed. In concert with certain social forces, they keep feeding our greed for sex and money, power and influence, control and excessive security, food and drink.

Their voices insist that we not only continually need

more; we have an absolute right to it. After all, we are told, perfection consists in having it all and having the best of it all. We always deserve better. Enough is never enough and sufficient is never good enough. Only the best will suffice. Sharing is for fools. The truly wise person gets and keeps it all or only shares in order to gain.

Like Lust, neither Avarice, nor Gluttony, deals only with the obvious. Avarice is not just about wealth. Gluttony is not just about food and drink. Lust is not just about sex. All three are at work in a broad range of human activity. The workaholic is as much their victim as the alcoholic and the glutton.

The person who hoards time, talent and love is as avaricious as the one who hoards possessions. The one who hogs conversation is as gluttonous as the one who hogs food and drink. The person who lusts after power is as lustful as the one who lusts after sex. Each of these demons makes use of a corresponding weakness in human nature.

Primarily, Avarice feeds our innate fear for security while Lust and Gluttony cater to our drive for pleasure. They will encourage us to live only for the moment, convincing us that this really is all there is to life.

If we listen to them and follow their lead, we will have no room in our lives for anyone but ourselves. There will be no concern for any needs but our own. We will end up in a state of deadly loneliness and isolation cut off from all that could bring us real peace and happiness. Our inter-personal relationships will be seriously harmed, even destroyed. The care and concern involved in loving others will be quashed. Having captured us with a promise of paradise, they will then leave us in a living hell.

In his novel <u>The Brothers Karamazov</u>, the great Russian writer, Fyodor Dostoyevsky, tells the parable of the onion. It is a convincing description of the destruction and the sadness Avarice brings.

> Once upon a time, there was a peasant woman and a very selfish and wicked woman she was. And she died and did not leave a single good deed behind. The devils caught her and plunged her into the lake of fire. So her guardian angel stood and wondered what good deed of hers he could remember to tell God: "she once pulled up an onion in her garden," said he, "and gave it to a beggar woman."
>
> And God answered, "You take that onion then, hold it out to her in the lake, and let her take hold and be pulled out. And if you can pull her out of the lake, let her come to Paradise; but if the onion breaks, then the woman must stay where she is."
>
> The angel ran to the woman and held out the onion to her. "Come," he said, "catch hold and I'll pull you out." And he began cautiously pulling her out. He had just pulled her almost out, when the other sinners in the lake, seeing how she was being drawn out, began catching hold of her so as to be pulled out with her.
>
> But she began kicking them. "I am to be pulled out, not you. It is my onion not

yours." As soon as she said that, the onion broke. And the woman fell back into the lake and she is burning there to this day. So the angel wept and went away. (Karamazov, pp 423—424)

We find the same lesson in the following parable:

The land of a rich man produced abundantly. And he thought to himself: "What should I do, for I have no place to store my crops?" Then he said, "I will do this: I will pull down my barns and build larger ones, and there I will store all my grain and my goods. And I will say to my soul, Soul, you have ample goods laid up for many years; relax, eat, drink, be merry."

But God said to him, "You fool! This very night your life is being demanded of you. And the things you have prepared, whose will they be?" (Lk 12, 16 - 20)

On the surface, there seems to be nothing wrong with the man's, nor the woman's, decision. All they seem to be doing is taking reasonable and prudent steps to secure their future well-being. In reality, however, they are being unreasonably selfish. He will not share his wealth; she will not share her good fortune. They will keep it all. In the end, their selfishness will be their undoing - the source of his death and her unending pain.

When Jesus warns us that we "do not live by bread alone" he is telling us that our true happiness and well-being will not be found in acquiring and holding on to all the pleasures and goods of this life. We are created for more than that. (cf. Mt 4, 3 - 4)

The gaunt, pale face of the miser and the bloated body of the glutton are apt images of Avarice and Gluttony. There is no joy in either. Our response to their presence is repulsion and pity.

Unless they are constrained, the demonic trio, Lust, Avarice and Gluttony, will gradually and imperceptibly take over our behaviour. The control over our lives that they promised us will be subsumed by them. The end result will be an addictive and/or compulsive activity over which we will have no control, hate it as we will. Unless help is available and accepted, we will finally be consumed with self-loathing. Frequently and tragically, suicide will often be seen as the only solution to the self-hatred so intensely felt.

Rarely will one be able to free oneself from the grip of these demons without help. Help will often be needed as well to overcome the shame and self-disgust that often prevent one from even seeking help.

Professional counselling and therapy can be very useful and is often necessary. But holistic healing will require spiritual healing and growth as well. Seeing oneself and one's life through the eyes of faith will invariably compliment and enhance physical and psychological healing.

To quote the Dutch Evangelist, Corrie Ten Boom: "Faith is like radar that sees, through the fog, the reality of things, at a distance the human eye cannot see."

Everything assumes its proper perspective when we shine the light of faith on ourselves and our lives.

In the light of faith we see our true worth and the true purpose for our existence. We also see the same value and life-purpose in all others. We see ourselves and others as the Beloved of the Father, precious in his sight, valued for no other reason than that we exist. We come to know ourselves and others for what we really are: incarnations of the Father's unreserved love. We learn to see through the lies the demons tell us and arrive at that truth that makes us free.

The same result occurs when we shine the light of faith on our lives. Our perspective on life, its meaning and purpose, changes when we see ourselves as created, not for a relatively short period of time, but for an eternal existence, not for what we can achieve or acquire, but for love.

As we deepen our relationship with God, our interpersonal relationships take on new meaning and direction. Our love becomes purer. We grow in our ability to reach out to others. We are more receptive to their efforts to reach out to us. Our motivation grows healthier. We begin to see others, not as objects to be used, but as gifts of God to be treasured.

Life will then be geared not to getting and keeping selfishly, but also to sharing. We will then be on the road to that peace and joy that this world cannot give because we will be living in and out of genuine love.

Faith also gives new perspective to all created things. In its truth we will see ourselves as the stewards, the trusted guardians and managers of God's creation, not its owners, and certainly not its selfish despoilers. Our response to creation will then become one of reverence and respect. Our use of created things will reflect our call as responsible and grateful users. Our worry about future security will be tempered by the recognition of God's unfailing concern and care for us.

Having provided for ourselves prudently and to the best of our ability, we will trustingly leave the rest to God. We will have no need to hoard this world's goods. These reassuring words of Jesus will take on new life: "Look at the birds of the air; they neither sow, nor reap, nor gather into barns, and yet your Father feeds them. Are you not of more value than they?" (Mt 6, 26)

We will also be able to make our own this prayer of the psalmist: "Teach me, O Lord, the shortness of my life that I may learn wisdom of heart."

Saying that prayer with understanding and sincerity will enhance our conviction that this life is not all there is, that we do not live just for the moment but for eternity, that our value does not lie in honours and possessions, but in our uniqueness, giftedness and beauty.

Chapter 11: Envy

"This above all to thine own self be true; and it must follow, as the night the day, thou canst not then be false to any man."
Hamlet, Act III

Who do you want to be? A seemingly innocuous question, but one fraught with danger. It can easily be taken to mean "Who would you rather be?" Put that way, the question becomes one asked by Envy.

In everyday speech, it is common to use jealousy and envy as if they meant the same thing. They do not. The dictionary describes "jealousy" as the state of being "earnestly and anxiously suspicious; vigilant in guarding; anxiously watchful." What we are anxious about and vigilantly guarding are our possessions: our good name, our position, our material goods. We are "anxiously watchful" about these because we want to hold on to them. For the right or the wrong reasons, we don't want them taken from us. Jealousy, then, is the child of Avarice.

The dictionary definition of 'envy' is very different. Envy is: "selfish and unfriendly grudging in view of what another enjoys."

The demon Envy can operate on two distinct levels. One can look at what another has and long for it, but without hatred or ill will. At some time, we all give in to Envy on this level. There is nothing very dangerous in this in and of itself. Unless it is controlled, however, it can be the slippery slope to level two. This journey from one level to the other is short. One must be careful not to make it.

It is on this second level, however, that the demon Envy is truly destructive. When we operate on this level we not only long for what others have, we hate them for having it. We treat them with ill will. We are willing to destroy them—even kill them—in order to get what they have. On this level, Envy reveals itself as the child of Gluttony and Lust.

This aspect of Envy is the common stuff of plays, novels, and operas. Iago in Shakespeare's Othello and Uriah Heap in Dicken's David Copperfield are familiar examples of people who destroy others – mortally, or otherwise – in order to get what the other possesses.

The Bible is also full of examples of Envy at its worst: Cain who kills his brother Abel because God accepts Abel's gift and rejects his, King David who has Uriah killed so he can possess Uriah's wife Bathsheba, King Saul who tries repeatedly to kill David because he is envious of David's popularity with the people.

The hatred and ill will arising out of Envy does not have to be extreme, nor does it have to lead to the physical death of another. There are lots of ways to "kill" someone. Rumor, slander, innuendo, malicious gossip and so forth can "kill" as effectively as a gun or knife.

What is usually missed by people motivated by Envy is this: the envious tools they use are always two-edged swords. They destroy the user as well as the victim. No one can sling mud and escape being at least splattered, or coated, by it oneself. Even if this doesn't happen, acting from vicious envy can dangerously deepen one's self-loathing. Envy has a way of "eating up" the person it possesses.

What in our nature allows Envy to operate at its most destructive level? In some cases, the answer is sheer greed. One simply wants what another has badly enough to destroy the other. A more common answer, however, centres on discontent with one's self. Here one hears Envy shouting: "Look at yourself and see how deficient you are."

This statement echoes the voices of all those Significant Others who have compared us to someone else. It is particularly harmful if the other person is a sibling or someone with whom we are vying for another's love. We may grow to hate them because they have what we do not have. We may also loathe them because we judge them as undeserving of the gifts they have and incapable of using them well.

Envy also has a way of strongly spotlighting all that is missing in one's makeup. As a consequence, what one has by way of personality, talent, capabilities, good looks, etc., dims into insignificance. What results is a pathological rejection of who one is and an unhealthy hunger to be all one is not.

This pathological state can never bring peace. No matter how well one succeeds in becoming someone else, satisfaction will not follow. We kid ourselves if we think it will. The fact is that there will be no end to what we want to become. Having "become" this person, we will then want to become that person, then another person, then another and so on, unendingly. Envy is always at work. Enough is never enough. The grass is always greener on the other side. Someone will always have more than us.

Developing or reinforcing a sense of blessedness is the most potent weapon against Envy. This is probably the most difficult task any of us will ever undertake since it involves acknowledging truths about oneself that one finds hard to hear.

At the heart of blessedness lies the reality that one is the Beloved of God, the Chosen One. Accepting this truth is always an arduous task. For some, it can prove an impossible one as well.

Our world is full of people who question whether or not they should ever have been born. Their low self-esteem easily leads them to depression, despair, envy and all kinds of self-destructive states. Claiming our blessedness is often a life-long work.

Unless the messages we receive speak strongly to our self-value, seeing ourselves as Chosen and Beloved will be impossible. Our society and our Significant Others play a crucial role here when they persist in their efforts to pull us into the darkness of self-doubt, low self-esteem, self-rejection and depression. The self-negativity with which others can infect us can seriously damage, even destroy, any movement towards realizing our blessedness. It can also make claiming our blessedness a tiring, seemingly never-ending, even impossible quest.

However, our Significant Others play as vital a role in our self-valuing as they do in our self-deprecating. They can give us life, as well as destroy us. While our Significant Others can heighten our sense of blessedness by their positive reinforcement of our worth as persons, other people can never be the ultimate source of our sense of our blessedness. Like us, they too are limited and flawed. They cannot meet all of our needs no matter how much they love us. Nor is it realistic to expect them to be always there for us when and how we need them to be. In fact, since we are all mortal, the day will come when we will no longer be together with them in this life. The one permanent, constant and all-embracing being available to us all is that Eternal Being we call God. It is in the creating and sustaining love of God that we find the true source of our blessedness. "Only in God will my soul be at rest," sings the psalmist.

At some point in the eternity of time, God called each of us into existence. Before we even existed in the womb, God knew us intimately, as only one can that truly creates. He knit us together in that womb. In doing so he incorporated into our very being all we would need in order to accomplish the particular purpose for which he created us. We can be sure of that. It would be unthinkingly heartless and cruel of God to create any of us for a specific end and then deny us what we need to reach it. He who is Love incarnate simply could not do so.

Each of us then exists for a reason. Even those who are broken in body, mind or spirit are among us for our growth. They teach us compassion, that most important of all human attributes. They call us to growth in our understanding and exercise of love. In so doing, they call us out of our selfish and often narrow worlds. We can learn from them to be grateful for even the smallest of things, the most insignificant victories. In them, God gives us a great deal.

Those among us whose brokenness and flawedness is not so debilitating also exist for a purpose. In fact, there will be as many reasons for our existing as there are people. No two of us will exist for the same purpose. Our uniqueness will forever belong solely to each of us. It will never be duplicated or cloned. We may possess identical gifts, but the use of those gifts will be flavoured by a personal and unrepeatable uniqueness. No two of us will ever sing or dance, design or create identically.

There is, then, no valid reason why one should succumb to Envy. The talents and abilities God has given each one are adequate to fulfill the purpose for which we were created. Whether they are greater or lesser than those of others is simply of no consequence. They are what each needs, no more and no less. God has entrusted them to us. Our task is to develop them and use them for good. Wasting our lives in detesting the comparative inadequacy of our own gifts, as well as envying those of another, is the useless and destructive work of Envy and an insult to God.

In fostering this destructive tendency to compare, Envy has a strong ally. We live in a society heavily based on comparison and fueled by competition. We want only the best and only the best will win or at least be worthy of our attention. So we compare everything: physical appearance, income, houses, children, everything. And our tendency to compare and compete produces winners and losers and only feeds Envy. It also destroys, or, at the very least, severely cripples our support systems. No one can work effectively with another when Envy rules. "Team-work" remains either a farce or a dream. Only when we acknowledge our weaknesses and strengths and those of others can we complement one another and work together for the good of all.

In summary then, the anger and resentment to which Envy gives birth blind us to the strengths we do have. Failure to value the strengths we have only adds to our discontent, our self-devaluing and depression. To live wholly, we must never let the things we cannot do stop us from doing the things we can do. We must learn to be happy doing however much or little lies within our God-given abilities. Then, with contentment and peace, leave the rest to someone else. Knowing where to go is as important as getting there.

"The eye is the lamp of the body. So, if your eye is healthy, your whole body will be full of light; but if your eye is unhealthy (envious), your whole body will be filled with darkness. If then the light in you is darkness, how great will that darkness be! Besides, which of you, by fretting over it, can add even one inch to your stature?" (Mt 6, 22 - 23; 26)

Chapter 12: PRIDE

"Let the one who boasts, boast in the Lord."
(1 Cor 1, 31)

My dictionary gives two contrasting definitions of pride. Each has its own validity.

The first of these is one we know well. "Pride: Undue sense of one's superiority; inordinate self-esteem; arrogance or superciliousness." It is this Pride that is universally condemned and numbered among the Seven Capital Sins.

For centuries Pride was seen only in this light. It was treated as the deadliest of all sins, the personification of evil. There was no "positive side" to Pride.

In part, this approach was due to our spiritual history as it was passed on to us in numerous works on spirituality. It has also been the consistent approach to Pride in traditional theology. Many of us grew up knowing only this one-sided, negative Pride.

It is a side of Pride that is very much a part of who we are and that makes it all the more dangerous. Whenever something that is natural in us runs out of control, suffering will follow. On both a personal and a global scale we have come to know well the destruction that results when sinful Pride runs wild.

Those who live with a sense of undue superiority rob us of our dignity and sense of self worth. They are quick to let us know that we can never measure up to them. Our ideas will never be as good as theirs. Our work will never equal what they can do. We will never be as good looking, as talented or efficient as they. Their motto is very simple: "Bow down you peasants and drink deeply from my largesse. You can never make it on your own."

Those who live in inordinate self-esteem say much the same thing. In their own estimation, they too are always better than anyone else. They may not rob others of their own self-esteem, but they will certainly bring it into question. They command undying respect and preferment and heaven help those who do not proffer it. The sad irony is that inordinate self-esteem is not really self-esteem at all. It is simply another disguise for Pride or Envy. People with solid self-esteem do not need to diminish others.

In our society, there are many people living their lives out of this inordinate self-esteem. All too often, however, their claim to the respect and deference they demand of us is not based on themselves as persons, but on acquired wealth, position, "celebrity status," etc.

Those who live convinced of their own superiority or undue self-esteem do a lot of harm to themselves and to others. Their contempt for others they consider inferior leaves them loveless and friendless. For them, those who are inferior exist only to pander to their self-glorification.

Their supposed care and concern for those they regard as equal or superior is also self-serving. They will value these relationships only for as long as they themselves somehow profit from them.

The too proud and arrogant often end up as victims of Envy as well as Pride.

None of us ever "has it all." There will always be someone else whose wealth, intelligence, prestige, etc., we must have, if we are to maintain our sense of superiority.

Pride may also be at work in the frenetic activity consuming so many of us.

There are those among us who consistently drive

themselves to operate beyond the level of their natural talents and abilities. They have a morbid fear of failure. Even worse, their self-value is based excessively on what they can do rather than who they are. Any shortcoming that becomes known by others is a major embarrassment. Minor mistakes are treated as major catastrophes. Even the smallest negative reaction threatens them with the loss of the recognition and approbation they need in order to keep going.

People in this sad state are possessed by obsessive perfectionism. They live out of a fear born and fed by Pride. Having vested their worth in achieving recognition or power or position, they are driven to hang on to it no matter what the cost to themselves or others. They exult in their glory and constantly demand that others exult in it as well. This demand for perfection creates enormous strain and stress, both for the perfectionist and those in relationship with him or her. Only rarely will any persons or relationships involved in this state emerge unscathed.

Fortunately for all of us, there is also a positive side to pride. This side of pride is not only legitimate, but is also necessary to our spiritual and psychological well-being. It can be defined as: "a proper sense of personal dignity and self worth; honourable self-respect or self-congratulation; that of which one is justly proud."

This side of pride is vital for our growth. It gives us the confidence to take risks. It empowers us to reach beyond our fears and, ultimately, to dare to find intimacy in our relationships with God and others.

Tragically, and for much too long, Christian asceticism wrongly equated this form of pride with the work of the demon, Pride, and saw it as equally sinful.

This equation was strongly reinforced by the teachings of John Calvin and other Christian theologians, as well as by the extremes of the Puritans and other religious movements. Their over-emphasis on our sinful nature and inclination left no room for legitimate self-esteem or praise. They saw this legitimate pride as both sinful in itself and as the slippery road to rebellion against God. Even valid self-glorification was seen as imitating the angels who rebelled against God. In Christian mythology, their leader was Satan and their rebellion gave birth to Evil and the creation of Hell. So self-glorification was to be avoided at all costs. It was simply too dangerous. No good could come of it.

It has taken a long time for us in the Western world to counter that misguided approach and accept honest self-esteem as a necessary component of holistic well-being. In fact, many of us are still uncomfortable, even somewhat fearful, of honest self-esteem. We know that we have a right to be proud of ourselves, but we feel better if we flavour that pride with at least a small feeling of guilt. We know that it is good for us to take legitimate pride in what we accomplish. We feel better about it, however, when we respond by downplaying the value of what we do or by giving the credit to someone or something else no matter how insincerely.

Our phony responses, however, get us nowhere. Their phoniness is too transparent. False humility is never virtuous. We gain nothing when we lie about ourselves. Total honesty with ourselves is the road to healthy self-esteem. The healthiest response to a deserved compliment is always an honest "thank you."

In reality, those words of thanks are more than a response. They are the key to the boundary between sinful pride and legitimate self-esteem. The balance between these two is found in one's grateful honesty about the totality of one's being as well as the value of one's accomplishments. This is the balance bar between the work of the demon Pride and the cultivation of wholesome pride or honest self-esteem.

"I give you thanks, O God, that I am so wondrously, so awesomely made." These words of the psalmist have it right. True self-esteem begins with gratitude for one's very existence. Gratitude because one exists makes it possible to be grateful for who one is, warts and all. There is no profit in cursing the day you were born or in covering over who God made you to be. A daily and sincere "thank you" is the healthy response to one's existence and one's being.

When we are grateful for who we are, we can acknowledge our need for others without threat or fear. None of us is complete in our selves. Accomplishments, good or evil, are never solo affairs. We do indeed need one another.

Realizing this truth is key to our gratitude both for our own gifts and the gifts of others. If we are honest with ourselves, we know that we need them and they need us. This complement of gifts is absolutely necessary both for reaching our human potential and for accomplishing what we wish to accomplish.

This mutual interdependence is part of God's design. It is a deep expression of our need for intimacy and community. God has designed his creation as an integral whole with Himself as its chief source and creator. We exist to further that design, not to alter or destroy it. But, we are not designed to live or to act alone. We need others in order to become and to do. We are not designed to be or to act in isolation. Our need for healthy intimacy is endemic to our human nature. We are designed to live in communion with others, not in separation from them.

These aspects of our humanness speak strongly of our need for others. We need them for who they are and who they can become. We need them for the gifts they bring to help us achieve our goals. And, for the same reasons, they need us.

The Judeo-Christian Scriptures stress this truth. Time and again we are reminded that each of us is essential to the welfare of the whole. Using the analogy of the human body, St. Paul reinforces that truth. To function properly, the body needs all its parts, each fulfilling its given role. The eye cannot be the ear, nor the ear the foot. One part cannot function for the whole. In order to be complete all parts must work together. Each must make its proper contribution.

> Indeed, the body does not consist of one member but of many. If the foot would say, "Because I am not the hand I do not belong to the body," that would not make it any less a part of the body. And if the ear would say, "Because I am not an eye, I do not belong to the body," that would not make it any less a part of the body. If the whole body were an eye, where would the hearing be? If the whole body were hearing, where would the sense of smell be? But as it is, God has arranged the members in the body, each one

of them, as he chose. If all were a single member, where would the body be?

As it is, there are many members, yet one body. The eye cannot say to the hand, "I have no need of you," nor again the head to the feet, "I have not need of you." On the contrary, the members of the body that seem to be weaker are indispensable, and those we think less honourable we clothe with greater honour, and our less respected members are treated with greater respect, whereas our more respected members do not need this.

But God has so arranged the body, giving the greater honour to the inferior member, that there may be no dissention within the body, but that the members may have the same care for one another. If one member suffers, all suffer together with it; if one member is honoured, all rejoice together with it. (1 Cor 12, 14 – 26)

We will do well to recognize the value of our need to be integrated in our own person and in our relationships. Living out of this will be a great help in our struggle with Lust, Envy and Pride. It is one thing to acknowledge our greatness and take all the credit for it. It is quite another to acknowledge it and give thanks for it.

We will do even better when we recognize God's role as the originator and the organizer of this healthy interaction. God is, after all, the ultimate source of all we are and all the good we do. He has given us our personhood and gifts in trust. With his guidance, we will be effective stewards.

"For it is God who works in you, both to will and to accomplish all you do." (Phil. 2, 13)

This reminder doesn't leave any room for inordinate pride.

Chapter 13: ANGER

"Lord, how often should I forgive? Seven times? No, not seven times but seventy times seven times."
(Mt. 18, 21)

As I said earlier, our difficulty in dealing with our demons is compounded by their use of aliases. None has more than Anger.

Like Pride, Anger masks its sinful self with aliases that are not only non-sinful, but necessary to our well-being.

In the light of this, it is important to remember that there is an essential difference between feeling anger and living out of anger.

There is no sin in the anger we feel in the face of injustice, of the abuse and exploitation of our environment, our labour, our possessions and ourselves. These are the feelings of justified or righteous anger. They are both positive and necessary. They are directed to correcting wrongs and establishing the good. They are warning signals, alerting us to the danger of the destruction and harm these sins bring to others and ourselves.

These feelings of anger can be very intense. They energize us. They can override our fear and hesitation in the face of needed action. Without them, injustice would go unchallenged and uncorrected. They can benefit both ourselves and our world.

This is the anger Jesus feels when he drives the moneychangers from the temple, when he berates the corruption of certain Pharisees, when he angrily corrects his own disciples.

It is important to remember, however, that this justified anger is a feeling, an emotion. Like all emotions, it must be controlled. Without control, this anger becomes its own monster. Instead of correcting injustice, it will create it own havoc.

When used properly, this anger will have two characteristics. Like all violent passions, it will be relatively brief. It will also create a lasting determination to work calmly and persistently to correct the wrong against which it is directed.

Only recently, however, are we beginning to accept the distinction between righteous anger and demonic Anger and actions resulting from righteous anger are still seen as sinful by some. Even the feeling itself is seen as morally wrong. In reality, however, our emotions automatically respond to stimuli whether or not we want them to.

Saying one must never get angry is demanding the impossible. Like it or not, emotions respond. The most one can do is try to control the response.

There are times, too, when an injustice is perceived and not real. This is particularly true when our anger is directed against God whose love for us is presented as always seeking our good. It is not always easy and often impossible to see what good there can be in the death of a child, a crippling accident, the loss of a job, the destruction of a career, etc.

In these situations, we feel betrayed. God has abused our love. Our emotional response kicks in and we feel angry with God. Simultaneously, that anger often brings with it feelings of fear and of guilt. Because of that, instead of facing that anger and working through it, our response is to suppress it. If we never work to change that response, it will seriously harm our relationship with God. We must come to accept that this fear and guilt are false emotional responses. Emotional anger towards God is as acceptable and as unavoidable as it is towards any other whom we see as betraying our love.

It doesn't matter whether the injury is real or simply perceived. The anger response will be equally intense and equally unavoidable. Only when we have allowed the waves of our indignation to pass over us will we find the good behind the tragedy.

While emotional anger is natural, necessary and healthy, existential anger is none of those. Existential anger is living anger. Its expression is either cold, calculating revenge, or fiery rage. Either it plots the destruction of its victim with cold, efficient detachment, or it strikes out indiscriminately and viciously. In both cases, it possesses and runs those in whom it lives.

Once again we are not speaking here of feeling angry, but of being angry. Existential anger is not the sudden and passing rush of emotional anger, no matter how intense that emotional response may be. Existential anger resides in the deep recesses of the psyche. It is a spiritual and psychological cancer. Like all cancer, it works its destruction whether or not the host is aware of its existence. And, like all cancer, its presence may become known only when its destruction becomes obvious.

If this living anger is the cold, calculating kind, its revengeful plotting will be patient and constant. Its source will be injustice, real or perceived, personal or more general. The one it possesses will be obsessed with revenge. No form of what it perceives as just retribution will be beyond it, no matter how repulsive, how sinful that act may be in itself. Inner peace is attained only when the obsessive thirst for vengeance or revenge is in some way satisfactorily satiated.

In its turn, existential anger in the form of rage is the result of adverse life experiences that seriously impair, or worse, totally destroy, one's sense of self worth. These experiences arise from interaction with those in one's life who are significant others. As we noted earlier, their role is vital and inescapable. Their influence confers the title "Beloved", which gives one life, or "Rejected", which brings death.

Rage may be directed at oneself or someone in one's present or past life. Its intensity will depend on the degree to which one's self-esteem has been damaged and the amount of time the rage has had to develop. When it has reached its apex, even the slightest provocation may cause it to erupt. Unless the situation is clearly understood, what provoked the rage is often mistaken as its cause. Not knowing the real cause results in baffling bewilderment: "Why did I blow up over that? "Why am I so irrationally angry over such a small thing? I removed the provocation, so why am I still angry?" This self-talk often serves only to increase the rage already present.

Psychologically, rage induces depression. Depression is rage turned inward against the self. The severity of the depression will be proportionate to the intensity of the rage. If sufficiently severe, the depression can result in the taking of one's own life or that of another. In any event, the fire of rage will always consume one's inner peace and contentment, in whole or in part.

Existential anger is also destructive spiritually. Its effects are fertile ground for the work of the demon. His efforts show themselves in the havoc he creates in ourselves and in our relationships. He urges us to respond to this anger by bitterness and inordinate resentment directed at ourselves as well as others. He will blind us to the damage our brokenness will inevitably do to all of our relationships, including our relationship with ourselves and with God.

Demonic Anger will urge us to courses of action that will promise solutions, or at least some relief. He will be lying to us yet again. The addictive use of drugs and alcohol will only increase the pain. Sexual wantonness will not bring freedom. It will only imprison us more in guilt.

Unless he is dealt with, Anger will join forces with Lust, Envy and Pride. Their combined strength will be too strong for us to fight. Our destruction will be complete.

The only effective antidote for rage is forgiveness. The problem is that forgiveness itself brings it own baggage. Some of that baggage is inherent in the forgiving process. Some has been added by misunderstanding.

The inherent baggage revolves around two points: dealing with one's past and the need for self-forgiveness. Rage is generally the result of one's past. The shame, mistakes, failures, cruelty, guilt and fear of past sins never die. Once done, the deed is forever embedded in the memory where it remains alive. It surfaces repeatedly in one's imagination, one's reveries, and one's dreams. Like it or not, we all do "have a past." Try as we might to dismiss it, or bury it, our sin is indeed always before us. And so too, the shame, guilt and fear it causes in us.

Our fear is that someday we may have to pay for our past, in this world or the next. We are well aware that individuals and society can be very unforgiving. Sexual abuse, deceit and deception, swindling and treachery for example are sins that can scar us for life. Fear of public exposure can paralyze us in the face of life or career decisions, in establishing relationships, etc.

For some, this fear of the past is focussed on the after-life. The horror of what they have done impacts them so strongly that they lose all hope of salvation. If they continue to believe in it at all, God's love for them becomes simply a matter of intellectual assent. It never reaches the heart. It has no real impact on the fear. Convinced they are damned, they live in despair. Consumed by shame and guilt, they know no peace.

If it is difficult for others to forgive us it can be even more so for us to forgive ourselves. Reflection on our past often leads to self-recrimination instead of self-forgiveness. When our past blocks our ambition or our love, we wonder how we could have done such a stupid thing. We become angry with ourselves. We rage at our weakness. We deny the deed, hoping that by denying it we can make it disappear. We blame the person or the circumstance and hope that this will exonerate us. We live in self-delusion in place of self-truth.

These negative responses may temporarily alleviate our feelings of fear, shame or guilt. They will not diminish or erase them. They will not bring the inner peace we seek. They are poor substitutes for the self-forgiveness, which alone can bring healing.

The road to self-forgiving begins with the honest admission of one's guilt. We cannot forgive what we refuse to acknowledge. The absence of guilt removes the need for forgiveness. Denying one's guilt may bring temporary comfort. In the long run, it accomplishes nothing. Admitting that one has sinned through one's own fault may be difficult but it removes a major roadblock on the way to self-forgiveness.

Truly forgiving oneself also demands honest self-disclosure and full acceptance of that self as it really is. To hate one's weakness is to hate an indispensable and valuable part of oneself. Denying one's tendency to sin is deadly self-delusion. It lulls us into a false sense of perfection. In doing so, it denies us the healing we need.

It is not easy to treasure our weaknesses in a world that glorifies strength. It is very difficult to be comfortable with our flaws when society places such strong and unrelenting emphasis on perfection. In such an atmosphere, weakness is not valued. It is derided, ridiculed, treated with shame, and often with guilt. We are mystified by the fact that someone like St. Paul could write that he gloried in his weakness, could be thankful for it and could find strength in it. Those words seem completely incomprehensible, if not somewhat ridiculous, to the modern ear.

Paul's words, however, capture the value we should attach to our weakness. Paul is not glorying in his weakness as a source of his sin. He is glorying in it as the wondrous receptacle of love. We are neediest in our weakness. It is there that the love of God and of others can truly find us and love us into wholeness. It is our weakness, not our strength, that cries out for the comfort, concern and forgiveness of others. In our weakness we cry out our need for the other. In their strengths, they can compensate for our lack. In the resulting union, we find that oneness that is both the beginning and the end of all true love.

When we have learned to cherish our weakness, we can begin the process of self-forgiveness. There will be no further need for false excuses. We can honestly acknowledge our sin. We can admit our deficiencies. We can begin our healing. We will no longer need to rage at ourselves.

The process of self-forgiveness also demands that we rethink a time-honoured misconception. We have forged a strong link between forgiving and forgetting. We have not, however, clearly defined what this "forgetting" involves. We can be so affected by the sins we have done, and those others have done to us, that forgetting them is impossible. They have scarred us too deeply. Telling us that we must forget them or forgiveness will be impossible presents us with a devastating dilemma. It denies us the forgiveness we need and the healing that forgiveness can bring. It simply victimizes us further.

The fallacy of that "truth" compounds its harm. Not only is it not necessary to forget in order to forgive, it is also dangerous. Forgetting one's past can indeed be the road to repeating it. Recalling the pain and harm of things past is an effective buffer against the folly of repeating them or allowing them to be repeated. The psychology inherent in the Alcoholic Anonymous movement strongly reflects that truth. It constantly reminds its members that they are always "recovering" alcoholics.

What is required here is the dissipation of the anger we feel, especially towards those who have abused us. Forgiving them does not require us to adopt them as bosom companions. It is sufficient that we reach the point where we can wish them a blessing instead of a curse. It also requires that, while we keep the memory, we refuse to live out of it. Laying aside our past and pressing on to what lies ahead is always a healthy way to diffuse our anger.

Learning to forgive oneself, then, is essential to the forgiving process. Until one has learned to do so, at least to some degree, it is impossible to receive forgiveness from God or anyone else.

No one is more forgiving of our weaknesses than God. He knows only too well of what stuff we are made. No one is more understanding than He. No one is more saddened by our sin than God. No one is more concerned for our well-being. No one weeps more profusely as we smash our beauty against the rocks of our wanton desires and anger. No one forgives us so completely, so tenderly, with such searching, such longing. No one sorrows more over the punishment our sin inflicts on ourselves and our world. No one is more aware of the healing power of forgiveness.

"God is Love," says St. John. In his unselfish, constant love for us lies the root of God's unreserved forgiveness for our folly.

All of this is exemplified in Jesus: in the acts of forgiveness he extends, in the words he speaks. Sacred Scripture is filled with powerful examples of God's forgiveness. Nowhere is this better illustrated than in the three parables found in the fifteenth chapter of Luke's gospel: the lost sheep, the lost coin, and the lost son.

This last, the Parable of the Prodigal Son, would be better called the Parable of the Loving Father and the Self-righteous Son. It has much more to do with these two than with the self-destructive living of the prodigal. In this parable we find the total spectrum of forgiveness. The searching, longing and loving forgiveness of the father is set in startling contrast to the aloof, smug and unforgiving response of the elder son. The loving forgiveness of the one brings a new robe, a ring, a feast - new life. The cold, unforgiving attitude of the older brother accomplishes nothing. In every call to forgiveness of ourselves or others, we must decide which attitude we will adopt. In a very real way, our decision will carry with it life or death.

My personal paraphrase of the Prayer of St. Francis may be of help in making that decision: "If you seek love, live lovingly; if you seek forgiveness, live forgivingly; if you seek peace, live peaceably."

The importance God attaches to forgiveness is clear from these words of Jesus:

> So when you are offering your gift at the altar, if you remember that your brother or sister has something against you, leave your gift before the altar and go; first be reconciled with your brother or sister, and then come and offer your gift. (Mt 5, 23)

The import of Jesus' words is clear: forgiveness is the indispensable prelude to acceptable worship. St. John supports this truth with these unqualified words:

> Those who say, "I love God" and hate their brothers or sisters, are liars. If they do not love their brothers and sisters whom they see, they cannot love God whom they do not see. (1 Jn, 20)

Any reluctance, difficulty or pain those words may initially cause will be amply off-set by the peace they will bring and the joy that will follow when we do our best to heed them.

Chapter 14: Sloth

"Go to the ant, you lazybones; consider its ways, and be wise. Without having any chief or officer or ruler, it prepares its food in summer, and gathers its sustenance in harvest.
(Proverbs 6, 6)

My dictionary defines "sloth" as: "a disinclination to exertion; laziness." This is what we automatically think of when we talk about sloth.

A clear understanding of sloth, then, demands an immediate distinction between sloth and restfulness. In many minds the two words mean the same but they are really very different. There are times when restfulness is both good and necessary; laziness is neither.

For far too many of us, restfulness has disappeared. Our lives are in over-drive. We must always be "busy." Busyness is seen as the indispensable virtue. There is a strong tendency to think that there is something seriously wrong with people who are not continually occupied with some task or another.

There is no doubt that a decent amount of activity is good for our health: physical, mental and spiritual, no matter what our stage of life is. The problem lies with the extreme importance we have come to place on the need to be kept busy.

Sociologically, we have tied our self-worth to our productivity. Not having something to do generates strong feelings of guilt and worthlessness. Retirement, leisure time, disabling illnesses all threaten us. They rob us of our "doing" and so we begin to question our value as persons. They are in fact so frightening that we are driven to search desperately for something to fill the void they can create. To paraphrase an oft-quoted saying: "I am busy, therefore I AM." So to keep "busy" and "mean" something, retirees, for example, often become busier [and more stressed] than when they were employed. Even our leisure time has to be filled with activity.

Other factors drive us as well. The sometimes unreasonable demands of children and spouses, the demands of others with whom we are in relationships, co-dependent demands, demands arising from the damage inflicted by significant others, job and career demands, etc., can also drive us to run scared of "free time."

Some of us are also driven by our gluttony. We have to taste all life has to offer. Nothing must be missed. Avarice drives us too. It compels us to "get all we can." Time off is time wasted because "time is money." And Fear, Lust and Pride, each in its own way, can drive us to unjustified busyness.

All our demands can exhaust us and stress us to the breaking point. Air rage, road rage, rage at having to wait, fear of unemployment, etc. are all symptoms of mental and physical exhaustion and of social and emotional stress. Too many of us are so busy making our living that we have no time to live. We have no time for leisurely conversation, for quietly being with another. We seem to have forgotten that relationships are not built by doing, but by being together.

Our frantic rushing to and fro has also robbed us of time to wonder and to ponder. This loss is seriously harmful to our inner selves: our souls, our psyche. We have neither the time nor the peace of mind to marvel at beauty or to contemplate the meaning a word or gesture has in our life. The result is a tragic diminution of our creativity, our spirituality, even of our humanity. Increasingly we have become machines, geared only to production. For many of us, taking time to smell the roses is either a dream or a sad joke.

We need the time and freedom that leisure gives us to contemplate the purpose of our existence. We need to take time to stop and straighten our priorities. And we need to do so with peace of mind. Idle hands are not always the devil's workshop. Sometimes, they are the doors to God's voice.

We need, then, to learn to value leisure. Healthy living, physical, mental and spiritual, requires a firmly established balance between busyness and restfulness. We are not designed to live in a state of perpetual motion. Nor are we meant to aimless drift through life, following unthinkingly wherever the current takes us. There are times, however, when we are meant to float, to deliberately decide to allow life's current to carry us effortlessly and restfully for a time.

The sin of sloth, then, does not lie in legitimate recreation and leisure. Its root is a willful decision to live in a state of absolute, unbroken laziness.

People who choose to live in laziness are intrinsically self-centered and selfish. They exercise neither the will nor the desire to contribute actively to anything. The world owes them a living and they owe no one anything. They clog our welfare roles and abuse our charity. In so doing they harm the deserving poor. By robbing them of the aid they need, they make us suspicious of the legitimate claim the honestly poor have on our love.

The willfully lazy are found in every segment of society, every profession and every walk of life. They abuse positions of power and trust to get what they want because it is the easiest way to achieve their goals. They pay no attention to the evil around them unless they can somehow profit from it. Social injustice, environmental abuse and the effects of natural disasters have no impact on them. They do nothing to help the needs of others. They don't even want to hear about them. They have no interest in anything or anyone but themselves.

Their biggest sin, however, is the damage their laziness does to love. Slothful people are too lazy to make a commitment or to spend the energy required for loving. Any pretence of selfless loving ceases when it begins to cost some effort on their part. Others involved in their relationships are too often left bruised and seriously hurt.

This cold indifference to the needs of others is a sin, the same sin as that promoted by Lust, Gluttony, Avarice, and Pride. It is a total rejection of the command to love even as we are loved, and it is a serious abuse of human dignity.

There is another and equally important dimension to sloth that we need to explore. It is called "acedia" or "spiritual sloth." Its psychological equivalent would be "ennui." People suffering from this form of sloth are inordinately restless, listless. There is no joy in their lives, their chins are perpetually dragging on the ground and they have neither the desire nor the ability to pray. Any attempt to get them to be joyful and happy [to rejoice in God's love for them] is met with a blank stare and a shrug. It's not necessarily that they don't believe; they just don't care. If they pray at all, their prayer is simply an unwelcome duty.

As all truly slothful people do, the spiritually slothful take without gratitude. When they are forced to give, they do so reluctantly, grudgingly. If they pray at all, it will only be to demand what they want. If they serve at all, it will only be for their own gain. They worship themselves alone. They live lonely lives in the idolatry of self. The mantras of their worship are: So what? What the hell? Oh, yeah? In some very sad cases this idolatry is sustained by the abuse of drugs, alcohol, sex or all sorts of frivolous amusements.

Like all its sinful partners, Sloth exacts its price from those it possesses. It makes its victims pathologically self-protective, fearful of any expression of emotion, terrified of any show of vulnerability, frightened of taking any risk. The result is lives devoid of all the zest and excitement of living, lives that are hollow and unfulfilled. This void is filled with an indifference that has no room for concern about the suffering of others on either the local or the global scene and this indifference does enormous harm both to the individual and to all of us.

Sociologically speaking, Sloth removes the need for one's existence. The lazy are seen as unproductive and parasitical. Human society does not value those who refuse to provide for themselves. It has no patience with those who unjustifiably divorce themselves from its needs. They are simply an additional, unwelcome burden.

Sloth also violates the divine purpose for our existence. We are created by God "to cultivate the earth and bring forth its fruits." As God's stewards, we are to continue to develop the work God began at creation. We are to actively preserve and enhance the earth, to discover the secrets of the universe and use them for the good of all. Our call is to be active participants with God as he continues his creative work in our world and in us. Above all, we are to put into action God's redeeming and sustaining love. Our lives are to serve as signs of the transforming power of this love. Out of this love we are then called to be active instruments in God's work of leading society to the fullness of its redemption. Deliberate refusal to do so is a sin.

It is this sin that Jesus references in the steward parables. It is this sin that St. Paul condemns so harshly:

> Now we command you, beloved, in the name of our Lord Jesus Christ, to keep away from believers who are living in idleness and not according to the tradition they received from us. For even when we were with you, we gave you this command: Anyone unwilling to work should not eat. For we hear that some of you are living in idleness, mere busybodies, refusing to do any work. Now we exhort such persons and we command them in the Lord Jesus Christ to do their work quietly and to earn their own living. All of you must work willingly for the glory of God and the good of others. The love God shares with you, you must share with your brothers and sisters. In that way, God's glory will be magnified. (2 Thess 3, 6 – 13)

Paul's words are more than a strong condemnation of Sloth. They are also a strong defense against the work of this demon.

Chapter 15: Resurrection

"Unless a grain of wheat falls into the ground and dies, it remains only a single grain; but if it dies, it yields a rich harvest."
(John 12: 24)

Every major religion teaches that life on earth does not end with death. In one way or another, we are destined to continue in existence forever. Death is not the final focal point of human existence.

In Christian teaching, this truth finds its expression in our belief in resurrection, both the Resurrection of Jesus and our personal resurrection in Him and with Him and through Him.

As Christians, our entire lives are meant to be governed by and directed to this truth. Our resurrected state begins with our immediate resurrection after our death as we enter eternity, and finds its complete fulfillment with the resurrection of our bodies at the end time. We do not rise again only in the faces of our children or the memories of those whom we have known and have known us. Above all we rise with and in the Lord Jesus. This is the fundamental and central teaching of Christianity.

Our entire lives, however, are meant to be a reflection, a mirror of this truth. In other words, resurrection is meant to be an ongoing event in our lives and not something we simply wait for physical death to begin. Our lives are meant to be a time of continuing growth wherein we are consistently dying to our selfishness and sin so that God's love and goodness can be increasingly reflected in us and through us find its way into this world. We are called to die to sin that we might live in newness of life, a transformation that is meant to be repeated time and again as we go through this life.

We are a broken people living in a broken world. We know well the scourge of AIDS, the terrors of war, the ravages of greedy nations, the systemic sexual abuse of children and adults for profit and pleasure, the evil of modern economic and human slavery, the systematic abuse of natural resources and the environment, and so forth. In other words, we are all too familiar with the global effects of Lust and Avarice and Gluttony and the rest of this notorious list of sins.

This global brokenness in which we live adversely affects our personal brokenness in different ways.

Instead of seeking healing for our personal sin, we tend to plug it into the world's brokenness. Plugging personal gluttony into that of the world makes one's own gluttony less offensive, less destructive. Keeping one's job or "getting ahead" often demands complicity in the sins of the system. It is easy to excuse our cooperation in the work of Gluttony and Avarice, Lust and Sloth, when our livelihood or ambition is threatened. "Why fight it?" we ask ourselves. "You can't win anyway. It's the way things work. If you want to survive, go along."

In the end, it is always easier to join the forces of evil than it is to fight them, to allow oneself to be led into temptation than to flee. We have become very adept at democratizing our morality. We determine right and wrong by the majority decision.

Our will to resist what is destroying our world is also negatively impacted by the very magnitude of global sin. Its strength and pervasiveness daunt us. We often feel hopeless and helpless.

Many of us feel the same way in the face of our personal brokenness. Repeated failures highlight both our weakness and the strength of the demons within us. The futility of our effort eventually gives way to hopelessness. We stop all movement towards healing and we run from the concomitant suffering. We resign ourselves to defeat and defeat highlights our powerlessness.

Powerlessness can be a terrible thing. It can lead us to self-rejection. As it does so, we will be increasingly open to self-loathing. We begin to hate ourselves and the powerlessness we experience.

This negative approach to our powerlessness will never bring healing. For healing to begin, we must embrace our powerlessness and let it bring life. And we must do so with the patience and understanding that our healing demands.

Unfortunately, we live in a social environment that makes this very difficult. Our society values strength and abhors weakness. We are conditioned to regard weakness with disdain: a source of shame and guilt. It must be hidden or denied.

For healing to begin, we must overcome at least some of our social conditioning. We must first learn to curb the excessive impatience society has instilled in us. We need to relearn that substance takes time and patience with ourselves, with God and all others.

The second truth we must arrive at is that our powerlessness is not a curse, but a blessing in disguise. It creates an empty space in which the love of another can live and bring us newness of life. The paradoxical truth of powerlessness is that it confers power. It empowers us by its lack of power because it brings us into communion with others. It is the root of our sense of unity and belonging and the basis of that mutual exchange of strength and need that we call love.

It is this truth that St. Paul recognizes, understands and boasts about. It gives voice to his paradoxical statement that his strength is in his powerlessness. Paul doesn't see his weakness as a value in itself. Its value lies in the room it gives to the power of love. God's love embraces his weakness and makes it strong. It empowers him in his personal growth and in his ministry. It transforms him and enables him to love those he had been so determined to destroy. (cf. 2 Cor, 9, 10)

Like powerlessness, love is also a paradox. It brings joy and pain, acceptance and rejection. It calls us simultaneously to live in another and to die in ourselves. There is no escaping its transforming power once we embrace it.

Love is transforming because it continuously calls us to growth. In various ways, it urges (prods us) towards the fullness of all we were created to be. Growth is always accompanied by suffering. It requires us to die to something within ourselves in order that a newness might take root in us. When it is born of love and guided by love, this death is the gateway to new life. Death is always the gateway to new life. Only when it dies can the seed bring forth a harvest.

As painful as this repeated cycle of suffering, death and resurrection can be, it is essential to our healing. It brings a blessing to our brokenness.

As Henri Nouwen writes in <u>Life of the Beloved</u>, "All addictions make us slaves, but each time we confess openly our dependencies and express our trust that God can truly set us free, the source of our suffering becomes the source of our hope." (p. 80)

This cycle has been an essential and life-giving part

of my life. Time and again I have had to take my brokenness to love to have it healed. This essential love has always been God's love for me, mediated through human love. I am very grateful for this love. Because of it, I had a constant surety that God was with me in those dying experiences of pain and darkness and loss of self. In some mysterious way, I knew that my pain was not a suffering unto death, but unto life. There was an assurance that there was value and purpose in my suffering, that in my brokenness, love had found me and brought me back to life once again. In the light of this love, I found hope. With the strength it gave me, I was able to control the demons that would destroy me.

None of us knows the complete map of a life journey. But I do know its outline. Our journeys will go from Galilee to Jerusalem to Calvary to Easter. Our hope lies in our ability to walk in the light and power of Jesus' Resurrection – of that marvelous and wonder-filled event so full of power that it brings order to chaos, life from death, light in our darkness and solace in our pain. In every resurrection moment and event, we are called to find the fulfilling of a basic need: the need to discover and to live our personal journey with faith and confidence, to be a person of hope even in the pain of our on-going creation, to trust that the death of suffering leads to birth into the newness of life.

The continuous death-resurrection cycle of our lives is meant to lead us little by little out of the pain of our darkness and despair and into the light of God's love for us – a light so strong that it illuminates our value. This value is so wondrous that God's Son became one with us and shared the pain and suffering, joy and wonder of human life. He became the Light and the Way leading us to that inner peace and self-fulfillment that alone is the true foundation of human peace and happiness.

We are called to follow Jesus in knowing His Father's love and acquiescing in love to His plan for our happiness. In this will lie the seeds of our own on-going resurrection here and the joy and peace of that final Resurrection that awaits us.

"In the Spring the song of the universe is heard again."
Winton Southern

APPENDIX I:

The Cup and the Potter
Unknown Author

There was a couple who used to go to England to shop in the beautiful stores. They both liked antiques and pottery and especially teacups.

This trip was to celebrate their twenty-fifth wedding anniversary

One day in a beautiful shop they saw a beautiful teacup. They said, "May we see that? We've never seen one quite so beautiful."

As the lady handed it to them, suddenly the teacup spoke. "You don't understand," it said. "I haven't always been a teacup. There was a time when I was red. And I was clay. My master took me and rolled and patted me over and over and I yelled out: "Let me alone." But he only smiled. "Not yet," he said.

"Then I was placed on a spinning wheel," the teacup said. Suddenly I was spun around and around and around. "Stop it! I'm getting dizzy!" I screamed. But the master only nodded and said: "Not yet."

Then he put me in an oven. I had never felt such heat. I wondered why he wanted to burn me and I yelled and knocked at the door. I could see him through the opening and I could read his lips as he said: "Not yet."

Finally the door opened. He put me on a shelf and I began to cool.

"There, that's better," I said.

Then he brushed and painted me all over. The fumes

*were horrible. I thought I would gag to death. "Stop it!
Stop it!" I cried.*

He only smiled and said: "Not yet."

*Then suddenly he put me back into the oven. It wasn't
like the first one. It was twice as hot and I knew I would
suffocate. I begged. I pleaded. I screamed. I cried. All
the time, I could see him through the opening, nodding
his head and saying, "Not yet."*

*Then I knew there wasn't any hope. I would never make
it. I was ready to give up.*

*But the door opened. He took me out and placed me on
a shelf. One hour later he handed me a mirror and said,
"Look at yourself."*

*And I did. I said, "That's not me; it couldn't be me. It's
beautiful. I'm beautiful."*

*"I want you to remember this," he said. "I know it hurts
to be rolled and spun around and seared in fire. But
look at the beautiful you that has emerged. Wasn't it all
worthwhile after all?"*

APPENDIX II:

Tommy

Father John Powell, a professor at Loyola University in Chicago writes about a student in his Theology of Faith class named Tommy: Some twelve years ago, I stood watching my university students file into the classroom for our first session in the Theology of Faith.

That was the day I first saw Tommy. My eyes and my mind both blinked. He was combing his long flaxen hair, which hung six inches below his shoulders. It was the first time I had ever seen a boy with hair that long. I guess it was just coming into fashion then. I know in my mind that it isn't what's on your head but what's in it that counts; but on that day I was unprepared and my emotions flipped. I immediately filed Tommy under "S" for strange . . . very strange.

Tommy turned out to be the "athiest in residence" in my Theology of Faith course. He constantly objected to, smirked at, or whined about the possibility of an unconditionally loving Father/God. We lived with each other in relative peace for one semester, although I admit he was at times a serious pain in the back pew.

When he came up at the end of the course to turn in his final exam, he asked in a cynical tone, "Do you think I'll ever find God?"

I decided instantly on a little shock therapy. "No!" I said very emphatically. "Why not," he responded, "I thought it was the product you were pushing."

I let him get five steps from the classroom door and then called out, "Tommy! I don't think you'll ever find

Him, but I am absolutely certain that He will find you!"
He shrugged a little and left my class and my life. I felt
slightly disappointed at the thought that he had missed
my clever line "He will find you!" At least I thought it
was clever.

Later I heard that Tommy had graduated and I was
duly grateful.

Then a sad report came. I heard that Tommy had
terminal cancer. Before I could search him out, he came
to see me. When he walked into my office, his body was
very badly wasted and the long hair had all fallen out as
a result of chemotherapy. But his eyes were bright and
his voice was firm, for the first time, I believe. "Tommy,
I've thought about you so often. I hear you are sick," I
blurted out.

"Oh, yes, very sick. I have cancer in both lungs. It's
a matter of weeks."

"Can you talk about it Tom?" I asked.

"Sure, what would you like to know?" he replied.

"What's it like to be only twenty-four and dying?"

"Well, it could be worse."

"Like what?"

"Well, like being fifty and having no values or ideals,
like being fifty and thinking that booze, seducing women,
and making money are the real biggies in life."

I began to look through my mental file cabinet under
"S" where I had filed Tommy as strange. (It seems as
thought everybody I try to reject by classification, God
sends back into my life to educate me.)

"But what I really came to see you about," Tom said,
"is something you said to me on the last day of class."
(He remembered!) He continued, "I asked you if you

123

thought I would ever find God and you said, " 'No!' "
which surprised me. Then you said, " 'But He will find
you.' " I thought about that a lot, even though my search
for God was hardly intense at that time.

(My clever line. He thought about that a lot!)

"But when the doctors removed a lump from my
groin and told me that it was malignant, that's when I got
serious about locating God. And when the malignancy
spread into my vital organs, I really began banging
bloody fists against the bronze doors of heaven. But God
did not come out. In fact nothing happened. Did you ever
try anything for a long time with great effort and with no
success? You get psychologically glutted, fed up with
trying. And then you quit."

"Well, one day I woke up, and instead of throwing a
few more futile appeals over that high brick wall to a
God who may be or may not be there, I just quit. I
decided that I didn't really care about God, about an
after life, or anything like that. I decided to spend what
time I had left doing something more profitable. I
thought about you and your class and I remembered
something else you had said: " 'The essential sadness is
to go through life without loving. But it would be almost
equally sad to go through life and leave this world
without ever telling those you loved that you had loved
them.' "

"So, I began with the hardest one, my Dad. He was
reading the newspaper when I approached him. Dad."

"Yes, what?" he asked without lowering the
newspaper.

"Dad, I would like to talk to you."

"Well, talk."

"I mean . . . it's really important."

The newspaper came down three slow inches. "What is it?"

"Dad, I love you. I just wanted you to know that."

Tom smiled at me and said it with obvious satisfaction, as though he felt a warm and secret joy flowing inside of him.

"The newspaper fluttered to the floor. Then my father did two things I could never remember him ever doing before. He cried and he hugged me. We talked all night, even though he had to go to work the next morning. It felt so good to be close to my father, to see his tears, to feel his hug, to hear him say that he loved me."

"It was easier with my mother and little brother. They cried with me, too, and we hugged each other, and started saying real nice things to each other. We shared the things we had been keeping secret for so many years.

"I was only sorry about one thing - that I had waited so long. Here I was, just beginning to open up to all the people I had actually been close to."

"Then, one day I turned around and God was there. He didn't come to me when I pleaded with Him. I guess I was like an animal trainer holding out a hoop, "C'mon, jump through. C'mon, I'll give You three days, three weeks."

"Apparently God does things in His own way and at His own hour. But the important thing is that He was there. He found me! You were right. He found me even after I stopped looking for Him."

"Tommy," I practically gasped, "I think you are saying something very important and much more universal than you realize. To me, at least, you are *saying that the surest way to find God is not to make Him a private possession, a problem solver, or an instant consolation in time of need, but rather by opening to love. You know, the Apostle John said that. He said: 'God is love, and anyone who lives in love is living with God and God is living in him.' Tom, could I ask you a favour? You know, when I had you in class you were a real pain. But (laughingly) you can make it all up to me now. Would you come into my present Theology of Faith course and tell them what you have just told me? If I told them the same thing it wouldn't be half as effective as if you were to tell it."*

"Ooh I was ready for you, but I don't know if I'm ready for your class."

"Tom, think about it. If and when you are ready, give me a call." In a few days Tom called, said he was ready for the class, and that he wanted to do that for God and for me. So we scheduled a date. However, he never made it. He had another appointment, far more important than the one with me and my class. Of course, his life was not really ended by his death, only changed. He made the great step from faith into vision. He found a life far more beautiful than the eye of man has ever seen or the ear of man has ever heard or the mind or man has ever imagined.

Before he died, we talked one last time.

"I'm not going to make it to your class," he said.

"I know, Tom."

"Will you tell them for me? Will you tell the world for me?"

"I will, Tom. I'll tell them. I'll do my best."

So, to all of you who have been kind enough to read

126

this simple story about God's love, thank you for listening. And to you, Tommy, somewhere in the sunlit, verdant hills of heaven - I told them, Tommy, as best as I could.

Rev. John Powell, Loyola University in Chicago

Bibliography

Scripture references and quotations: <u>the New Revised Standard Version</u>, Oxford Press Edition, 1977

<u>Seven Deadly Sins:</u> Campolo, Joseph. Wheaton Ill., Victor Books, 1987

<u>The Brothers Karamazov:</u> Dostoyevsky, Fyodor. New York: Random House, Inc., 1950

<u>The Other Six Deadly Sins:</u> Sayers, Dorothy. London: Methuen & Co., Ltd. 1943

<u>The Seven Deadly Sins:</u> Jewish, Christian and Classical Reflections on Human Nature: Schimmel, Solomon. New York: The Free Press, 1992

<u>Who Is This God You Pray To?</u>: Hayes, Bernard. Living Flame Press, New York, 1981

<u>Life of the Beloved:</u> Nouwen, Henri J.M. The Crossroads Publishing Co., New York, 1992

<u>Belonging</u>: Bonds of Healing and Recovery: Dennis Linn, et al. Paulist Press, Mahwah, N.J. 1993.

<u>Christian Spirituality in the Catholic Tradition:</u> Aumann, John. Sheed & Ward, London. Fourth impression. 1987.

<u>Spirituality and the Gentle Life:</u> Van Kaam, Adrian. Dimension Books, Denville, N.J., 1974

About the Author

Bernard Hayes is a Roman Catholic priest and a member of the Congregation of the Resurrection. He completed his theological studies at St. Peter's Seminary in London, Ontario and was ordained to the priesthood in 1957.

Following ordination, he completed additional studies at Laval University, Quebec City, Quebec; Fordham University, New York, New York; and the Pontifical Gregorian University, Rome, Italy.

He has served as a secondary school teacher and administrator and as president and rector of a seminary college. From 1977 to 1985 he was Associate Director of the Office for Spiritual Renewal for the Archdiocese of Louisville, Kentucky. From 1985 – 1993 he served as Director of Faith Development for the Waterloo Region Catholic School Board based in Waterloo, Ontario. In 1993 he was assigned to Rome to establish an International Centre for Resurrectionist Spirituality. On his return to Canada, he was assigned to St. Mary's parish in Kitchener, Ontario.

He currently lives in Waterloo, Ontario and continues to be involved in various ministries and several community organization and projects.

Additional Books by Bernard Hayes

To Live as Jesus Did

A treatment of the joys and sorrows, challenges and suffering of everyday life from a Christian perspective: How did Jesus deal with these life situations? How are we called to respond to them as Jesus' followers?

Who Is This God You Pray To?

A consideration of the various images of God: How do they affect our prayer? How can we move from negative to positive images of God?
(ISBN: 0-914544-41-1)

Love in Action

A commentary on chapters 14 – 17 of the Gospel according to John as a basis for lay ministry.
(ISBN: 0-914544-57-8)

These books can be ordered on-line at www.alibis.com.